Living Like St. Paul

From persecutor to believer, and the
lessons to learn from him

This book is dedicated to God first. He has blessed me with so much in my life and I must always give thanks for Him. Even when times are tough, He had my back.

Additionally, a HUGE thanks to my wife who comes along this journey with me with excitement, adventure and support, without which I would not be the man I am today.

Lastly to my daughter who took the time to help. Thank you for all that you have done and know that I will be here always for you.

Living Like St. Paul: A Guide to Christian Virtue

We always can find joy

Joy is a major theme of the New Testament. The word "joy" occurs 63 times and the word "rejoice" occurs 77 times. St. Paul didn't know what he was doing until he knew what he was doing.

"Always be full of joy."
1 Thessalonians 5:16

"But the fruit that the Spirit produces in a person's life is love, joy, peace, patience, kindness, goodness, faithfulness."
Galatians 5:22

"I pray that the God who gives hope will fill you with much joy and peace as you trust in Him. Then you will have more and more hope, and it will flow out of you by the power of the Holy Spirit."
Romans 15:13

We can all find joy regardless of what is going on and in general, if we really think about it, there is almost always something going on within our circle, could be to us personally or it could be in the world around us, to rejoice about.

In Nehemiah chapter 8, Nehemiah is reading the Scripture to God's people. They have fallen out of touch with God. They haven't heard His Word in a long time, and there are people who are helping them understand what God's word means. As Nehemiah and those assisting him bring understanding to the people about what God requires, the people begin to cry. They realized how badly they have missed the word and how far away from God they have drifted.

While all are sad and crying Nehemiah says to them, in Nehemiah 8:10, *Then he said to them, "Go your way, eat the fat, drink the sweet, and send portions to those for whom nothing is prepared; for this day is holy to our Lord. Do not sorrow, for the joy of the Lord is your strength."*

This last step in taking God's strength is the personal choice to have joy and rejoice. You have to choose to rejoice. Think about this, scripture tells us to rejoice in the worst of circumstances. You and I make a choice to rejoice because joy is not dependent on circumstances. We can have joy regardless of what is going on, and generally, if we really consider things, there is almost always something in our lives to rejoice about.

Consider Paul's situation in the first chapter of Philippians. He is chained up in jail, and he says, "Look. There are guys out there who are preaching Christ with the wrong motives. They are preaching Christ out of selfish ambition and greed, just to get something out of it." He said, "And they are doing it just to spite me, to try to make me more miserable in my bonds." Despite this, Paul said, "At least Christ is being preached, and in this I will rejoice." He is saying that even though the other motives may be way wrong, at least they are talking about Jesus. He found something to rejoice in. Right now, you may have unpaid bills, unruly children, or be sick of some sort. You don't rejoice *for* those things, but you can rejoice *in* those things. Rejoice because God has an answer, and you are not locked in, truly focused on the important things, if nothing else, rejoice that your name is written in the Lamb's Book of Life. Even on your worst day, you are still headed to heaven. When we choose to rejoice, God's strength comes. The joy of the Lord is our strength.

Here's the first activity for you to start with prior to reading the rest of this book. Write down the following prayer on a note card and keep it with you this week. Whenever your joy starts to waver and negative thoughts enter your head and occupy a space that they shouldn't, pull out your card and pray:

Heavenly Father, You said You meet him who rejoices, so help me choose joy. I realize that joy is not dependent on my circumstances. I can choose to rejoice because You know what I'm going through. You know how I'm feeling, and You desire to get involved. I trust You to do just as You have promised. Amen

Chapter 1: Introduction to St. Paul

In the story of human history, there are moments when a single life undergoes a profound transformation—a transformation that not only alters the course of that individual's existence but is heard throughout time, through the ages and shaping the destinies of countless others. Such an enormous transformation occurred on a dusty road to Damascus, where a man named Saul, later known as St. Paul, encountered the risen Christ. This encounter marked the beginning of a remarkable journey—a journey of faith, mission, and enduring legacy. Let's go back just a bit to the heart of ancient history, amidst the busy streets of Jerusalem, where a man named Saul stood tall, firmly rooted in his beliefs. His path was clear, his mission was strong and unwavering, but little did he know that the road ahead would lead him to a transformation so profound it would alter the course of human history.

Saul was not just an ordinary man of his time; he was a devout Jew, a Pharisee, and a passionate defender of traditional Jewish beliefs, a man of conviction. Born in Tarsus, a city with a rich cultural blend, he was brought up in a Jewish family that took pride in their heritage and faith. As he grew into adulthood, his passion for Judaism deepened, and he soon became a student of the famous Jewish teacher Gamaliel. Saul's devotion to Judaism was unmatched and he began to notice the growing movement known as "The Way" or Christianity and determined it a dangerous threat. He viewed the followers of Jesus as heretics who were undermining the religious traditions, the traditions that he held so close. He truly believed that the followers of Jesus, a growing movement in Jerusalem, were heretics threatening the very fabric of Judaism. Saul was determined to eradicate this perceived heresy, even if it meant using force.

It was on one fateful journey to the city of Damascus that Saul's life took an unexpected turn. As he traveled, a blinding light from the heavens surrounded him, and he heard a voice, a voice that would resonate through the ages. "Saul, Saul, why do you persecute me?" it asked. Saul, trembling and humbled, replied, "Who are you, Lord?"

"I am Jesus, whom you are persecuting," came the astonishing response.

In that moment, on the dusty road to Damascus, Saul underwent an astounding conversion. The man who once sought to destroy the followers of Jesus became one of the most fervent and dedicated apostles of Christ. The encounter with Jesus on that road forever changed the course of his life, and his influence on Christianity.

St. Paul's story is one of radical transformation, of faith discovered in the most unexpected of places. It is a story of redemption, of turning away from a life of hostility and persecution to one of love, compassion, and unwavering faith. His journey from Saul to Paul symbolizes the transformative power of faith and conversion that has the potential to touch every human heart. It serves as a reminder that no one is beyond redemption and that even the most zealous adversaries of the Gospel can become its most passionate champions.

In the pages that follow, we will explore the life, teachings, and enduring legacy of St. Paul. We will delve into the lessons he imparted through his letters to the early Christian communities and the lessons that continue to inspire and guide countless individuals today. It is our hope that by studying his life and following his example, we can learn how to live our lives in a way that reflects these same virtues.

As we take off on this journey to live like St. Paul, let us remember that our own paths may also be transformed when we least expect it. Just as Saul became Paul on that road to Damascus, we too can experience a change of heart and purpose. It truly is my hope that through this exploration of St. Paul's life and teachings that we all will be inspired to live lives of faith, love, and service, and may it bring us closer to the enduring message of Christ.

To understand the significance of St. Paul's conversion, we must look deeper into the historical and religious context of his time. Saul was living in a world that was a crucible of religious and political upheaval. The Roman Empire had extended its dominion over vast territories, including Judea, where Jerusalem was a center of religious and cultural significance. Saul was born in Tarsus, a city in the Roman province of Cilicia, sometime around AD 5-10. His birthright included Roman citizenship, a privilege that would later play a crucial role in his missionary journeys. However, it was not Saul's citizenship but his zealous devotion to Judaism that defined him in his early years. Saul belonged to the Pharisaic sect—a group of devout Jews known for their strict adherence to the Law of Moses and their dedication to preserving the purity of Jewish faith. He was trained as a Pharisee under the renowned Jewish teacher Gamaliel in Jerusalem. This education equipped him with a deep knowledge of Jewish law and tradition, making him a formidable scholar and debater. Saul's love for the Jewish faith was unyielding. He saw the budding Christian movement as a heretical sect that threatened the purity of Judaism. In this fervor, he actively persecuted early Christians, playing a prominent role in the stoning of Stephen, one of the first Christian martyrs (Acts 7:58-60). Saul's reputation as a persecutor of Christians spread fear among the followers of Jesus, leading to their dispersion from Jerusalem (Acts 8:1).

The Religious Landscape: Judaism, the faith of Saul's birth, was a complex era of religious sects and beliefs. The Pharisees, of which Saul was a part, were known for their strict adherence to Jewish law and traditions. They believed in resurrection, the afterlife, and the importance of following the Torah meticulously. The Sadducees, on the other hand, held more conservative views and rejected these beliefs. Meanwhile, the Essenes, or some of the Jewish people from that time, withdrew from mainstream society to pursue a greater development of self-discipline and communal lifestyles in the desert.

Amidst this religious diversity, a new movement emerged—the followers of Jesus of Nazareth, who claimed to be the Messiah. Initially, these followers were considered a sect within Judaism. However, their belief in the divinity of Jesus and the forgiveness of sins through his sacrifice began to set them apart.

As previously mentioned, one of the most notorious events in Saul's early life was his approval of the stoning of Stephen, a devout Christian who boldly proclaimed his faith. As Stephen was martyred, Saul watched over the cloaks of those who carried out the brutal act. It was a scene of violence and intolerance, and Saul played a prominent role in it.

The Road to Damascus - It was amidst this backdrop of persecution and violence that Saul set out on his journey to Damascus. He carried with him letters of authority from the high priest, granting him permission to arrest any followers of Jesus he encountered. Little did he know that this journey would lead to an encounter that would shake the core of his beliefs.

The blinding light that surrounded Saul on the road to Damascus was not just a physical phenomenon; it was a metaphor for the blinding light of divine truth that was about to pierce his heart and soul. Falling to the ground, he was confronted by a voice that asked, "Saul, Saul, why do you persecute me?" In that moment, Saul's life changed forever. When Saul asked, "Who are you, Lord?" the response he received was astonishing: "I am Jesus, whom you are persecuting." It was a revelation that would shatter his preconceived notions and transform his understanding of God, faith, and humanity. This encounter with the risen Christ was not merely a vision or a hallucination; it was a direct and personal epiphany. In that moment,

Saul realized the profound truth that Jesus, whom he had viewed as a heretic and a threat, was indeed the Messiah, the Son of God. It was a revelation that cut to the core of his being, challenging everything he had ever known and believed.

Literally blinded by the intensity of the experience, Saul was led into the city of Damascus by his companions. For three days, he neither ate nor drank, lost in deep reflection and prayer. It was during this period of physical blindness that he gained true spiritual sight. In a vision, Ananias, a devout Christian in Damascus, received a message from the Lord instructing him to go to Saul and lay hands on him. Ananias, initially reluctant due to Saul's reputation, obeyed the divine command. As Ananias laid hands on Saul and prayed for him, something remarkable happened. Saul's sight was restored, but more importantly, he was filled with the Holy Spirit. It was a symbol of his spiritual rebirth and empowerment for the mission that lay ahead.

Following his encounter with Ananias, Saul underwent an incredible change. He adopted the name Paul, a name that signified his transformation from persecutor to disciple. This change in name was symbolic of his change in identity and purpose. Paul's conversion was not a mere change of religious affiliation; it was a complete transformation of his heart, mind, and soul. The man who had once persecuted Christians with zeal now became one of their most ardent defenders. He shifted from being a persecutor to being persecuted, as he faced opposition, imprisonment, and hardships for the sake of Christ and the Gospel. The conversion of Saul to Paul holds immense theological significance. It highlights the universality of God's grace and the idea that no one is beyond redemption. Saul, a fervent persecutor of Christians, became Paul, one of the most influential figures in the history of Christianity. The man who once sought to eradicate the Christian faith became its most prolific writer and theologian. Paul's conversion also underscores the central message of Christianity—the transformative power of faith in Jesus Christ.

The Impact on Early Christianity: The conversion of Saul had a deep impact on the early Christian community. Initially, the followers of Jesus were wary of Paul, as they remembered him as the persecutor of their brethren. However, as they witnessed his fervor and commitment to the Gospel, they gradually accepted him as a fellow believer. Paul's conversion also opened doors for the Gospel to be preached to the Gentiles. While Peter and the other apostles primarily focused on the Jewish community, Paul saw his mission as taking the message of Christ to the non-Jewish world. He became known as the "Apostle to the Gentiles," and his missionary journeys would lead to the establishment of Christian communities throughout the Roman Empire. The road to Damascus is not just a historical event but also a symbol of transformation and awakening. It represents the journey from darkness to light, from ignorance to knowledge, and from hostility to love.

Questions to ask yourself about your transformation

These questions can help you clarify your intentions and goals as you start your religious transformation and provide a foundation for self-reflection and exploration.

1. What would it take for you to consider a religious transformation?
2. What aspects of your current belief system or religion no longer align with your personal beliefs or values?
3. How do you envision your relationship with the divine or the spiritual realm evolving during this transformation?
4. Have you shared your intentions regarding this transformation with your family and friends, and if so, how have they reacted?
1. How do you plan to navigate moments of doubt or uncertainty that may arise during your religious transformation?
2. In what ways do you hope your ethical and moral framework will evolve as a result of your transformation?
3. How will your religious transformation impact your daily life, including your relationships, career, and lifestyle choices?
4. How will you engage with and learn from the broader religious or spiritual community as you embark on this transformative journey?
5. Have you experienced challenges or conflicts with family and friends due to your evolving religious beliefs?

6. How has your sense of purpose or meaning in life shifted as a result of your religious transformation?

7. Do you feel a greater sense of connection or disconnection with the natural world because of your transformation?

8. In what ways has your religious transformation influenced your daily life, including your relationships, career, and lifestyle choices?

9. How do you envision the future of your religious or spiritual journey, and what goals or aspirations do you have related to it?

Chapter 2: Faith and Conversion

As mentioned in chapter 1, Saul, a man whose commitment to persecuting Christians was unwavering, encountered a blinding light and a voice from heaven that marked the beginning of a journey that would lead Saul to become the apostle known to us as St. Paul. We explored the world of Saul, the religious landscape of his time, and the intense persecution he spearheaded against the early followers of Jesus. We witnessed the astonishing moment when Saul, struck by a blinding light, heard the voice of Christ Himself asking, "Saul, Saul, why do you persecute me?"

In this chapter, we will dig deeper into the themes of faith and conversion, examining how this transformative encounter on the road to Damascus reshaped Saul's life and set the stage for his extraordinary journey as St. Paul.

Saul's life up to the moment of his encounter with Christ was marked by unwavering faith—in the religious traditions of Judaism, in the righteousness of his cause, and in his own understanding of God's will. His commitment to these beliefs was so strong that he was willing to use violence to suppress any perceived threats. But the road to Damascus was a sincere moment of crisis for the faith of Saul. The blinding light that surrounded him and the voice from heaven shattered the certainty in all the beliefs he had held. In an instant, the foundations of his religious convictions were shaken, and he found himself questioning everything he thought he knew.

Before we study Saul's crisis of faith, let's truly understand the nature of faith itself. Faith, in its most fundamental sense, is a deeply personal and spiritual commitment to a set of beliefs or values. It is the bedrock upon which individuals build their understanding of the world, their purpose in life, their relationships with others and their relationship with God. Faith is often interwoven with a combination of factors, including upbringing, cultural influences, personal experiences, and the teachings of religious or philosophical traditions. It provides a framework for interpreting the world and offers answers to questions about existence, morality, and the afterlife. In the case of Saul, his faith was deeply intertwined with his identity as a Pharisee and his upbringing in Jewish traditions. His commitment to these beliefs was strong, even unwavering, and he saw himself as a defender of the purity of Judaism against what he perceived as heretical influences. Saul's crisis of faith began with the blinding light that enveloped him on the road to Damascus. In that moment, the certainty he had held about his mission and his understanding of God's will was shattered. The voice from heaven asked, "Saul, Saul, why do you persecute me?" It was a question that cut to the core of his beliefs. This crisis was not merely intellectual; it was existential. Saul's encounter with Christ challenged the very essence of his identity and purpose. He was confronted with the realization that the one he had seen as a heretic and a threat was, in fact, the Son of God.

A crisis of faith is obviously a deeply personal and often stormy experience. This type of experience shatters one's deepest beliefs and catapults all they know into oblivion and with it comes a new way of not just thinking but being. It can take various forms, from doubts and questioning to a complete upheaval of one's beliefs. Several factors contribute to such crises:

a) Cognitive Dissonance: When an individual's beliefs and experiences are in conflict, cognitive dissonance arises. Saul had to reconcile his previous convictions about Jesus as a threat to Judaism with the revelation that Jesus was divine.

b) Emotional Turmoil: A crisis of faith can evoke intense emotions, including fear, confusion, guilt, and anger. Saul, who had been zealous in his persecution of Christians, likely felt profound guilt and remorse.

c) Reevaluation of Beliefs: Individuals in crisis often reevaluate their beliefs and the evidence that supports them. Saul had to revisit his understanding of Scripture and the teachings of the prophets considering his encounter with Christ.

d) Seeking Answers: A crisis of faith often prompts individuals to seek answers through prayer, reflection, and dialogue. In Saul's case, he spent three days in Damascus, neither eating nor drinking, engaged in deep reflection and prayer.

While crises of faith can be deeply challenging, they also have the potential to be extremely transformative. They invite individuals to examine their beliefs with fresh eyes, to explore new perspectives, to open their minds to faith and inspiration and to deepen their understanding of the divine. Saul's crisis of faith was transformative in the truest sense. It led him to reevaluate not only his beliefs about Jesus but also his entire worldview. It set him on a path of profound spiritual discovery and ultimately, to becoming one of the most influential figures in the history of Christianity.

The road to Damascus is not just a historical event but also a powerful metaphor for the human experience of faith and conversion. It symbolizes the journey from spiritual blindness to enlightenment, from hostility to love, and from ignorance to knowledge. Before his encounter with Christ, Saul was spiritually blind. He saw Jesus and His followers as threats to the religious traditions he held dear. His understanding of God's will was clouded by the zeal of his convictions. In our own lives, spiritual blindness can take many forms. It prevents us from seeing the divine in unexpected places, from recognizing the sacred in the ordinary, and from embracing the fullness of God's love and grace. The road to Damascus challenges us to examine our own spiritual blindness and to seek the enlightenment that comes from a deeper relationship with the divine. It invites us to open our hearts and minds to new possibilities, to question our assumptions, and to be receptive to moments of profound revelation.

Saul set out on that road with the intent to persecute and arrest the followers of Jesus. His heart was filled with animosity and anger. Yet, in an instant, his encounter with Christ redirected his path toward love and compassion. Conversion experiences often involve a shift from opposition to empathy, from division to unity, and from judgment to acceptance. Saul's conversion reminds us that even those who appear as adversaries can undergo an enormous change of heart and become agents of love and reconciliation. In our own lives, we are called to examine the areas where hostility may reside and to seek the transformative power of love. The road to Damascus challenges us to look beyond our preconceived notions and to recognize the divine image in every human being, even in those we may regard as enemies.

Another aspect of the road to Damascus metaphor is the journey from ignorance to knowledge. Saul's encounter with Christ was a moment of transformative revelation, where the depths of divine wisdom were unveiled to him. Ignorance, in certain circumstances, is not merely a lack of information but a resistance to deeper truths. Saul, in his zeal, had been ignorant of the teachings of Jesus and the message of love, forgiveness, and salvation that truly is the root of the Gospel. The blinding light on the road to Damascus shattered his ignorance and opened the door to a world of spiritual knowledge. In our own lives, ignorance can manifest as a limited perspective, a lack of empathy, or a failure to seek wisdom beyond the surface. The road to Damascus encourages us to embark on a lifelong quest for knowledge and understanding of ourselves, others and of the divine. It reminds us that moments of enlightenment can occur when we least expect them, often in the midst of our ordinary journeys and often in the midst of the pain. It calls us to be receptive to these moments, to seek wisdom from various sources, and to continually deepen our understanding of the mysteries of faith and existence.

Conversion, in the context of faith, is a radical transformation of one's beliefs, values, and way of life. It involves a turning away from a previous state of being, often characterized by sin, ignorance, or spiritual blindness, and a turning toward a new path of righteousness, enlightenment, and divine alignment. The story of Saul's conversion to Paul embodies the essence of conversion. It is a story of repentance and redemption, of an incredible change of heart, and of a commitment to live in accordance with God's will. Saul's encounter with Christ was not just a change of religious affiliation; it was a complete reorientation of his identity and purpose.

Repentance is a central theme in Saul's conversion. It is the recognition of one's shortcomings, sins, and errors, followed by a sincere desire to turn away from them and seek forgiveness. Saul, who had been an active persecutor of Christians, was confronted with the enormity of his actions and the need for repentance. Repentance is a universal theme in religious and spiritual traditions. It is a recognition of our human imperfections and a call to seek reconciliation with God. Saul's repentance set the stage for his redemption and transformation into St. Paul.

Conversion often involves a change of heart—a shift in one's desires, priorities, and values. His heart, once filled with hostility, was now filled with love for God and for his fellow human beings. This change of heart is not merely a psychological transformation but a spiritual one. It was an alignment with the divine will and a commitment to live in accordance with the teachings of Christ. In Paul's case, it meant a life of service, sacrifice, and unwavering faith.

Conversion is not a one-time event but an ongoing process of living in alignment with God's will. St. Paul's life after Damascus was marked by a relentless commitment to spreading the Gospel, nurturing Christian communities, and living out the principles that he had once persecuted. Living in alignment with God's will requires a deepening of one's relationship with Him, a commitment to spiritual growth, and a willingness to follow the path of righteousness, even in the face of challenges and hardships. Paul's life exemplified this commitment, and his letters to the early Christian communities continue to provide guidance for believers seeking to do the same. The story of Saul's conversion to Paul holds a universal message for all of humanity. It reminds us that no one is beyond redemption, that moments of transformation are possible, and that faith has the power to reshape our lives in remarkable ways. In our own journeys of faith, we may encounter moments of crisis, doubt, and questioning. We may wrestle with spiritual blindness, ignorance, or hostility. We may not understand the situation or even see a way out of it. Yet, the road to Damascus beckons us to remain open to the possibility of conversion—to be receptive to moments of enlightenment, to seek the transformative power of love, and to embrace the path of righteousness.

Saul's transformation into St. Paul offers a plethora of lessons and insights for our own faith journeys. Let's explore some of these lessons and how they can be applied to our lives today.

> ***The Power of Divine Grace:*** Saul's conversion is a powerful testament to the transformative power of divine grace. It illustrates that no one is beyond the reach of God's love and mercy. Saul, who had been a persecutor of Christians, was chosen by Christ Himself for a remarkable purpose. This lesson reminds us that God's grace is boundless and can bring about prolific changes in the most unexpected ways. It challenges us to extend grace and forgiveness to others, recognizing that they too may be on their own journeys of transformation.

The Role of Personal Encounters: Saul's encounter with Christ on the road to Damascus was a deeply personal and direct revelation. It serves as a reminder that personal encounters with the divine can be catalysts for change. While not everyone may experience a blinding light and a voice from heaven, moments of divine encounter can occur in various forms—through prayer, reflection, scripture, or the wisdom of spiritual mentors. This lesson encourages us to cultivate a receptive heart and a listening ear, open to the possibility of encountering the divine in our own lives. It invites us to seek moments of communion with the sacred, where we can be transformed and renewed in our faith.

The Role of Repentance and Forgiveness: Saul's repentance was a pivotal step in his transformation. It teaches us that acknowledging our own shortcomings and seeking forgiveness is an essential part of the spiritual journey. Repentance is not a sign of weakness but a testament to our capacity for growth and change. This lesson invites us to reflect on our own lives and consider where we may need to seek forgiveness or extend forgiveness to others. It emphasizes the importance of reconciliation and healing as integral aspects of the faith journey.

The Call to Service and Sacrifice: After his conversion, Paul's life was marked by service and sacrifice. He endured hardships, persecution, and imprisonment for the sake of the Gospel. His example reminds us that faith is not a set of beliefs but a call to action—a call to love, serve, and sacrifice for the well-being of others. This lesson challenges us to live out our faith through acts of kindness, compassion, and service to those in need. It underscores the idea that faith is not passive but active, and that it calls us to be agents of positive change in the world.

The Quest for Knowledge and Understanding: Saul's transformation was not just a matter of the heart but also of the mind. He delved into the scriptures, engaged in theological debates, and sought to deepen his understanding of the faith. His letters to the early Christian communities are filled with theological insights and reflections. This lesson encourages us to cultivate a hunger for knowledge and understanding in our faith journeys. It reminds us that faith and intellect are not at odds but can complement each other. We are called to be lifelong learners, continually seeking to deepen our understanding of the mysteries of faith and existence.

Embracing Change and Growth: Perhaps one of the most enduring lessons from Saul's transformation into St. Paul is the idea that change and growth are integral to the human experience. Saul's journey from a zealous persecutor to a devoted apostle reminds us that we are not bound by our past actions or beliefs. We have the capacity for transformation and renewal. This lesson invites us to embrace change and growth in our own lives. It challenges us to be open to the possibility of transformation, even when it seems unlikely. Just as Saul became Paul on the road to Damascus, we too can experience profound moments of renewal and redirection in our faith journeys.

The story of St. Paul's conversion is not merely a historical narrative; it is a living testament to the enduring power of faith, transformation, and divine grace. As we reflect on the lessons from Saul's journey, we are called to consider how we can live like St. Paul in our own lives today. There are so many distractions in today's world that you really must determine if your words and actions are focusing on the world we live in or on His world. "While we may not expect blinding lights and voices from heaven, we can create space in our lives for divine encounters. This means setting aside time for prayer, meditation, and reflection—moments when we open ourselves to the presence of divine intervention. It also involves seeking opportunities to encounter the divine in unexpected places, in the faces of strangers, and in the beauty of nature or in the silence of contemplation. St. Paul's transformation was marked by a shift from hostility to love. We are called to follow in his footsteps by cultivating hearts of compassion and empathy. This involves seeing humanity in others, even those with whom we may disagree or have conflicts. It means extending love and understanding, even in the face of adversity. Repentance and forgiveness are essential aspects of the faith journey. We are called to examine our own lives and seek forgiveness when needed. We are also called to extend forgiveness to others, recognizing that we all make mistakes and have the capacity for change. Forgiveness is a pathway to healing and reconciliation. St. Paul's life was marked by sacrificial love and service. We are called to emulate his example by seeking opportunities to serve others, especially those in need. This can take many forms, from volunteering in our communities to supporting charitable causes. Service is an expression of love in action. The quest for knowledge and understanding is a lifelong endeavor. We can follow in St. Paul's footsteps by delving into the scriptures, engaging in theological exploration, and seeking wisdom from diverse sources. Knowledge deepens our faith and equips us to engage with the complexities of the world. Finally, we are called to embrace change and growth in our faith journeys. This means being open to the possibility of transformation, even when it challenges our existing beliefs or perspectives. It involves a willingness to learn from our experiences, to adapt to new circumstances, and to continually seek a deeper relationship with the divine.

The story of St. Paul's conversion on the road to Damascus serves as a timeless testament to the power of faith and transformation. It reminds us that our faith journeys are not fixed or static but dynamic and evolving. Just as Saul became Paul, we too can experience moments of profound renewal and redirection in our lives, guided by the enduring message of faith, love, and divine grace.

The enduring legacy of St. Paul extends far beyond his personal transformation and the communities he nurtured in the early days of Christianity. His writings, teachings, and example continue to shape the faith and practice of millions of Christians around the world. St. Paul is often referred to as the "Apostle to the Gentiles" for his pivotal role in spreading the message of Christ beyond the Jewish community. His missionary journeys took him to diverse regions of the Roman Empire, where he established Christian communities and shared the Gospel. Paul's emphasis on the inclusion of Gentiles in the Christian faith laid the foundation for the universality of Christianity. His letters, addressed to these early communities, continue to offer guidance and theological insights that resonate with believers of all backgrounds. St. Paul's writings, found in the New Testament, are a rich source of theological reflection. His letters to various communities, such as the Romans, Corinthians, and Galatians, address a wide range of theological and ethical topics. Some key theological contributions include:

Justification by Faith: St. Paul's teachings emphasize that individuals are justified (made righteous) through faith in Christ rather than by adherence to the Jewish law. This belief, coupled with acts of faith has had a universal impact on Christian theology and the understanding of salvation through faith.

The Body of Christ: St. Paul's metaphor of the "body of Christ" illustrates the interconnectedness of believers within the Christian community. This concept underscores the idea that each member has a unique role and contributes to the well-being of the whole.

Love as the Greatest Virtue: In his famous discourse on love in 1 Corinthians 13, St. Paul elevates love as the greatest virtue. His words continue to inspire Christians to cultivate love, compassion, and selflessness in their lives.

Resurrection of the Dead: St. Paul's teachings on the resurrection of the dead offer hope and assurance of life beyond this earthly existence. His reflections on the nature of the resurrection have deeply influenced Christian eschatology.

St. Paul's ethical teachings, rooted in the love and moral principles of Christ, continue to guide Christian conduct. His emphasis on virtues such as love, faith, hope, and humility provide a moral compass for believers seeking to live out their faith in daily life. His practical advice on issues like marriage, relationships, and community life remains relevant to contemporary Christians, offering insights into how to navigate the challenges of today while remaining faithful to Christian values.

St. Paul's life and legacy are remarkable, his example provides a roadmap for how we can live meaningful and faithful lives in our own contexts. What can we remember about his life and teachings?

Embrace Transformation: St. Paul's transformation from Saul to Paul reminds us that change is possible, even in the most unlikely circumstances. Embrace moments of transformation in your own life, whether they come through encounters with the divine, challenges, or personal reflections. Be open to reevaluating your beliefs and values when faced with new insights.

Cultivate Love and Compassion: St. Paul's emphasis on love as the greatest virtue underscores the central importance of love in the Christian faith. Cultivate love and compassion in your interactions with others. Seek to understand and empathize with those around you and extend acts of kindness and generosity.

Pursue Knowledge and Understanding: St. Paul's commitment to deepening his understanding of the faith serves as a model for lifelong learning. Engage in the study of Scripture, theology, and philosophy. Seek wisdom from diverse sources and engage in meaningful conversations that challenge and expand your perspectives.

Live Out Your Faith*:* St. Paul's life was marked by action and service. Live out your faith by serving others, whether through volunteering, acts of charity, or supporting those in need. Put your faith into action by embodying the principles of love, forgiveness, and justice in your daily life.

Persevere in Faith: St. Paul's perseverance in the face of adversity serves as a testament to the strength of faith. In times of challenge or uncertainty, hold fast to your faith and remain resilient. Trust in the divine plan and remember that your faith journey may involve trials that ultimately lead to growth and transformation.

As you navigate your own path, be open to divine encounters, embrace moments of transformation, and seek to live a life of faith, love, and service. Just as St. Paul's legacy endures through the ages, your own journey of faith may leave a lasting impact on those you encounter, reflecting the transformative power of divine grace.

Questions to ask yourself about faith and conversion

These questions can provide you with a framework for self-reflection and exploration as you navigate your journey of faith and conversion.

1. What does faith mean to you, and how do you define it in your life?

2. How has your understanding of faith evolved over the years?

3. Are there specific life experiences that have strengthened or challenged your faith?

4. What role does faith play in your daily decision-making and actions?

5. How do you balance faith with reason and critical thinking in your life?

6. Have you ever experienced a crisis of faith, and if so, how did you navigate it?

7. What beliefs or principles do you have the most faith in, and why?

8. How does faith relate to your sense of purpose or meaning in life?

9. How has your faith influenced your relationships with others, including family, friends, and your community?

10. What is the role of doubt and skepticism in your faith journey?

11. Have you explored different religious or spiritual traditions, and if so, what have you learned from them?

12. How do you handle religious or philosophical differences between yourself and others in your life?

13. How does your faith influence your ethical and moral decision-making?

14. Have you ever felt that your faith was tested by challenging life circumstances, and how did you respond?

15. How do you envision the future of your faith journey, and what goals or aspirations do you have related to it?

16. In what ways does your faith shape your perspective on the world and your place in it?

Chapter 3: The Ministry of St. Paul

Let's talk about the ministry and trace the journeys of St. Paul, whose travels and teachings back then continue to inspire and instruct believers to this day. Let's look at where he went, how he inspired others, the differences he made along those trips and determine just how it all relates to us today.

We'll begin in the Roman Empire, where religious diversity was the norm. People worshiped a wide variety of gods and goddesses from various traditions, including the Roman, Greek, Egyptian, and local deities. Mystery cults and philosophical schools also pushed for followers. The religious atmosphere was overcrowded to say the least. Amidst this religious diversity, Judaism held a unique position. Jews, though a minority, were found in many cities throughout the empire. Their monotheistic faith and distinct practices set them apart from the polytheistic majority. It was out of this religious environment that Christianity emerged, initially as a sect within Judaism. The early Christian community was small and vulnerable, yet it possessed a powerful message—the message of Christ's life, death, and resurrection, and the promise of salvation through faith in Him. This message resonated with both Jews and non-Jews, offering hope and meaning in a world filled with uncertainty and persecution. St. Paul, originally a persecutor of Christians, became one of the most influential figures in this emerging faith. We've already thoroughly discussed his conversion, on the road to Damascus, as detailed in Chapter 2, and this marked a turning point not only in his life but in the trajectory of Christianity itself.

St. Paul's first journey is a testament to his unwavering commitment to spreading the Gospel. It laid the foundation for subsequent journeys and established Christian communities in key cities of the Eastern Mediterranean. This was recorded in the New

Testament of the Bible, particularly in the Book of Acts. It began in the city of Antioch, a busy metropolis in ancient Syria. Antioch was not only a center of trade and commerce but also a huge hub of early Christian activity. It was from this diverse and bustling city that St. Paul, along with Barnabas and John Mark, otherwise known as Mark the Evangelist, set out on their journey. Barnabas, whose birth name was Joseph and had the nickname "Barnabas," meaning "Son of Encouragement," by the apostles because of his positive and supportive nature, played a crucial role, especially in the mission to the Gentiles. He was instrumental in bringing Paul, the former persecutor of Christians, into the fold of the Christian community in Jerusalem and vouched for his conversion (Acts 9:26-27). The missionary trio's first destination was the island of Cyprus, Barnabas's place of birth. They began this ministry in Salamis, a prominent city on the eastern coast of the island. St. Paul, known for his persuasive speech and his knowledge of Scripture, preached in Jewish synagogues, declaring Jesus as the fulfillment of the messianic prophecies. From there, their journey across Cyprus took them to Paphos, where they encountered a significant challenge in the form of a Jewish sorcerer named Bar-Jesus (Elymas). This confrontation resulted in the conversion of Sergius Paulus, the Roman ruler of Cyprus; a pivotal moment in their mission. From Cyprus, St. Paul and his friends sailed to the mainland of Asia Minor (modern-day Turkey) and arrived in Perga. They then made their way inland to Pisidian Antioch, a city nestled in the rugged terrain of the Anatolian plateau. In Pisidian Antioch, St. Paul delivered a pivotal sermon in a synagogue. In this sermon, he traced the history of salvation through the Hebrew Scriptures, proclaiming Jesus as the fulfillment of God's promises. This message resonated not only with Jews but also with a significant number of God-fearing Gentiles. However, their success in Pisidian Antioch also stirred opposition from some Jews who were envious of their influence. This opposition led St. Paul and his companions to move on to the neighboring cities of Iconium and Lystra. Iconium and Lystra were both cities in the region of Lycaonia. In these cities, St. Paul and his companions faced both acceptance and opposition. In Iconium, they continued to preach in synagogues and gained followers among both Jews and Gentiles. However, fierce opposition from Jewish leaders forced them to flee to Lystra. In Lystra, St. Paul performed a notable miracle when he healed a man who had been lame from birth. The local population, amazed by this miracle, began to regard Barnabas as Zeus and St. Paul as Hermes, the gods of Greek mythology. St. Paul and Barnabas vehemently rejected these claims, emphasizing their own humanity and the message of the one true God. Despite the positive response from the crowds, trouble arose once again when Jews from Antioch and Iconium arrived and stirred up opposition. St. Paul was stoned and left for dead outside the city. Miraculously, he survived, and he and his companions continued their journey. The first missionary journey concluded with a return to Antioch, the city from which they had initially departed. St. Paul and his companions gathered the believers and reported the miraculous conversions and challenges they had encountered during their travels. This journey had lasting significance as it demonstrated that the message of Christ was not limited to a single geographical location but could transcend cultural and religious boundaries.

The success of St. Paul's first missionary journey raised significant questions for the early Christian community. These questions would be addressed in a gathering of leaders known as the Council of Jerusalem. One of the central questions confronting the early Christian community was the status of Gentile converts to Christianity. Did they need to fully convert to Judaism, including circumcision and adherence to the Jewish law, before becoming Christians? This question arose in the wake of St. Paul's successful outreach to Gentiles during his missionary journey. To address this issue, leaders from the Christian community in Jerusalem convened a council. The meeting, often referred to as the Council of Jerusalem, happened in 49 or 50 AC and was a significant moment in the history of Christianity. The central issue that led to the Council of Jerusalem was the question of whether Gentile believers needed to adhere to the Jewish law, including practices like circumcision, in order to be considered part of the Christian community. St. Paul and Barnabas, along with other delegates, made their way to Jerusalem to present their case.

At the council, St. Peter, who had experienced a divine revelation regarding Gentile conversion (as recounted in Acts 10), testified to God's inclusion of Gentiles into the Christian community. He emphasized that God had purified the hearts of Gentile believers through faith, and he cautioned against imposing the Jewish law on them. After much debate and discussion, St. James, known as "James the Just" and the leader of the Jerusalem church, delivered a decision. He proposed that Gentile converts should not be burdened with the full weight of Jewish law and customs but should adhere to a set of basic requirements, including abstaining from idolatry, sexual immorality, and the consumption of blood. This decision marked a significant theological development within Christianity. It affirmed the inclusion of Gentiles without requiring them to become Jews first. It also emphasized the importance of faith in Christ and living out a life in accordance with Christian ethical standards. The decision of the Jerusalem Council had far-reaching implications for St. Paul's missionary work. It affirmed his approach to Gentile conversion and removed a significant obstacle to his ministry. It also laid the groundwork for the continued expansion of Christianity beyond Jewish communities.

The Second Missionary Journey (50-52 AD): With the resolution of the Gentile conversion issue, St. Paul took off on his second missionary journey. This journey would take him to new regions and presented both opportunities and challenges. The second missionary journey began with St. Paul and Barnabas intending to revisit the cities where they had established Christian communities during the first journey. However, a disagreement arose over whether to take John Mark with them. St. Paul was hesitant due to John Mark's departure during the first journey, while Barnabas wanted to give him another chance. This dispute led to a separation, with Barnabas taking John Mark and setting sail for Cyprus, while St. Paul selected Silas as his companion and journeyed through Syria and Cilicia.

St. Paul's journey through Asia Minor led him to strengthen the existing Christian communities and establish new ones. He visited the cities of Derbe and Lystra, where he encountered Timothy, a young disciple with whom he would develop a close relationship. From there, the journey took them to Phrygia and Galatia, regions where St. Paul had previously ministered. It was during this time that the Holy Spirit guided them not to preach in Asia (western Asia Minor) and Bithynia (northern Asia Minor), leading them to the city of Troas. In Troas, St. Paul received a significant vision—a man from Macedonia pleaded with him, saying, "Come over to Macedonia and help us." Taking this vision as divine guidance, St. Paul and his companions set sail for Macedonia, marking a pivotal moment in the expansion of Christianity into Europe. Their first stop in Macedonia was the city of Philippi. It was here that St. Paul encountered Lydia, a businesswoman who became one of the first converts in Europe. He also cast out an evil spirit from a slave girl, leading to opposition from her owners and his eventual imprisonment. While in prison, St. Paul and Silas sang hymns and prayed, resulting in a miraculous earthquake that opened the prison doors. Acts 16:16-40: "Suddenly there was an earthquake, so violent that the foundations of the prison were shaken; and immediately all the doors were opened and everyone's chains were unfastened." Paul and Silas were also imprisoned while preaching by the Romans. The jailer, witnessing these events, came to faith in Christ along with his household. Leaving Philippi, St. Paul and his companions arrived in Thessalonica, where they preached in the synagogue. Some Jews and many Gentiles believed in their message, but opposition from Jewish leaders forced them to leave the city. They continued to Berea, where they found a more receptive audience among the Jews. However, opponents from Thessalonica followed them to Berea, prompting St. Paul to move on to Athens while Silas and Timothy remained in Berea. Athens, the renowned center of Greek philosophy and culture, presented a unique context for St. Paul's ministry. He engaged in debates with philosophers in the marketplace and addressed the Athenian council, the Areopagus, where he introduced them to the "unknown God" they worshiped. St. Paul's message in Athens emphasized the concept of the one true God and the resurrection of Jesus. While some Athenians mocked him, others were intrigued and believed. Among his converts were Dionysius the Areopagite and Damaris.

St. Paul's journey eventually led him to the city of Corinth, a bustling trade center and a crossroads of diverse cultures. Here, he met Aquila and Priscilla, a Jewish couple who had recently arrived from Rome due to Emperor Claudius's edict expelling Jews from the city. St. Paul worked with them as a tentmaker and established a close friendship. Corinth became a significant center for St. Paul's ministry. He preached in the synagogue, and Crispus, the synagogue leader, along with many Corinthians, believed and were baptized. However, not all Jews agreed with him so he faced some opposition. Due to this, he declared that he would turn to the Gentiles. During his time in Corinth, St. Paul experienced notable encouragement from the Lord in a vision. The Lord assured him that he would not be harmed, and that there were many people in Corinth who belonged to Him. This divine reassurance served as a source of strength and fortitude as St. Paul continued his ministry in Corinth, remaining there for a significant period.

The Third Missionary Journey (53-58 AD): St. Paul's third missionary journey continued his efforts to strengthen existing

Christian communities and extend the reach of the Gospel. This journey would also bring many challenges. The third missionary journey began with St. Paul's arrival in the city of Ephesus, a major center of trade and culture in Asia Minor. Ephesus was another significant location for St. Paul's ministry during this journey. He encountered a group of disciples who had received the baptism of John but were not aware of the Holy Spirit. So by the power of the Holy Spirit, he laid hands on them and they received the Holy Spirit demonstrating the transformative power of the Gospel.

St. Paul also spent two years in Ephesus, teaching daily in the lecture hall of Tyrannus. His ministry there was marked by miraculous healings and conversions. People brought their magic scrolls and occult books and publicly burned them, symbolizing their commitment to Christ.

While St. Paul's ministry in Ephesus was fruitful, it also stirred up opposition from those whose livelihoods were tied to the worship of the goddess Artemis. A silversmith named Demetrius, fearing a decline in the demand for Artemis-related crafts, instigated a riot against St. Paul and his companions. The riot, fueled by economic concerns posed a significant threat to St. Paul's safety. However, the local authorities eventually calmed the situation, and St. Paul continued his ministry in Ephesus before eventually departing.

Leaving Ephesus, St. Paul embarked on a journey through Macedonia, revisiting the Christian communities he had previously established. His time in Macedonia and Achaia (southern Greece) was marked by exhortations to the believers, the collection of contributions for the impoverished Christians in Jerusalem, and preparations for his eventual journey to Jerusalem. St. Paul's journey brought him to the coastal city of Miletus, where he summoned the elders of the Ephesian church for a farewell address. This poignant speech, recorded in Acts 20, encapsulated his ministry's ethos and values. He recounted his unwavering commitment to proclaiming the Gospel, despite numerous trials and hardships. In his farewell, St. Paul expressed his willingness to face more trials and suffering for the sake of the Gospel. He emphasized his role as a witness to God's grace and urged the elders to shepherd the flock faithfully, warning of future challenges to the church. The third missionary journey concluded with St. Paul's return to Jerusalem, a city fraught with tension and political volatility. Despite the warnings of impending danger, St. Paul was determined to complete the mission entrusted to him—the delivery of the contributions from the Gentile churches to the impoverished Christians in Jerusalem. Upon arriving in Jerusalem, St. Paul faced opposition and was arrested by Jewish authorities who accused him of defiling the temple and stirring up trouble among the Jews. He was imprisoned, setting in motion a series of legal proceedings that would eventually lead to his appeal to Caesar and a journey to Rome. St. Paul's imprisonment in Jerusalem marked a significant turning point in his ministry. He would spend several years in custody, facing trials and adversity, yet continuing to bear witness to the Gospel before governors, rulers, and even King Agrippa.

 St. Paul then journeyed to Rome, not a planned missionary journey but a consequence of his arrest and appeal to Caesar. However, this journey would become a crucial chapter in his life and ministry. St. Paul's journey to Rome began with his transfer from Jerusalem to the coastal city of Caesarea, where he would await transport to Rome. While in Caesarea, he was placed under the custody of the Roman governor, Felix. After appealing to Caesar, St. Paul was set on a journey by sea to Rome, accompanied by a Roman centurion named Julius and other prisoners. This sea voyage, recounted in Acts 27, was marked by challenges, including a shipwreck on the island of Malta. The ship sailed from the port of Caesarea and encountered rough seas, making the journey very dangerous. Despite Paul's warnings about the dangers of continuing the voyage, the centurion in charge and the ship's owner decided to press on. As the ship battled the stormy weather, it eventually lost control and was driven across the Adriatic Sea. The situation grew increasingly dire, with the crew and passengers fearing for their lives. It was at this point that an angel of the Lord appeared to Paul, reassuring him that he would reach Rome safely and that all those on board would be spared. After fourteen days of being battered by the storm, the sailors sensed that land was near. One night, they found that the water was getting shallower so, fearing that they might run aground on rocks, they dropped four anchors and waited for daybreak. When daylight came, they saw land but did not recognize the place. They decided to run the ship aground on the beach. The ship eventually struck a sandbar or a reef, and the waves began to break the vessel apart. The soldiers on board planned to kill the prisoners to prevent any from escaping, but the centurion wanted to save Paul, so he ordered that those who could swim should jump overboard first and make their way to land. The rest were to follow on planks or pieces of the ship. In the end, all those on board, including Paul, made it safely to the shore of an island. The natives of the island, whom tradition identifies as the Maltese, showed them unusual kindness by providing warmth and hospitality. According to Acts 28:11-16, Paul and the other survivors spent three months in Malta, where they were treated hospitably by the locals. They eventually boarded another ship, an Alexandrian ship with the Twin Brothers as its figurehead, which had wintered in the island. This ship had likely come to Malta for trade. The ship sailed to various ports in the region, including Syracuse in Sicily, where they stayed for three days. From Syracuse, they continued their journey and arrived at Rhegium, and after a day, a south wind came up, allowing them to reach Puteoli. In Puteoli, Paul and his companions found believers and stayed with them for seven days. From Puteoli, they traveled by land to Rome, and when the believers in Rome heard about Paul's arrival, they went out to meet him at the Forum of Appius and the Three Taverns. This meeting was a source of encouragement for Paul.

Upon arriving in Rome, St. Paul was placed under house arrest. He continued to preach and teach while in custody, welcoming all who came to see him. He wrote several of his Epistles (letters) during this period, including Ephesians, Philippians, Colossians, and Philemon. St. Paul's imprisonment in Rome allowed him to reach a diverse audience, including members of the imperial household. His message of Christ's salvation reached even into the heart of the Roman Empire. St. Paul found himself caught in the web of imperial power. Charged with offenses related to his unwavering Christian beliefs and unwavering missionary endeavors, Paul faced a trial that would ultimately lead to the culmination of his earthly journey. The trial, is a pivotal moment in the narrative of St. Paul's martyrdom. As a Roman citizen, Paul would have been afforded certain rights, including the opportunity to face his accusers. The charges against him were not just legalistic but also bore the weight of religious and political implications.

Sentenced to death, St. Paul faced the inevitable with a steadfastness born of unwavering faith. The method chosen for his execution, beheading, was considered more humane for Roman citizens, a concession of sorts for one who had traveled the reaches of the empire in the name of Christ. History tells us that after the sword fell and severed the tie between body and soul, St. Paul miraculously stood and continued to preach briefly. This miraculous act, symbolic of his unyielding dedication to the Gospel, has become a cherished element of the narrative surrounding his martyrdom. The place of St. Paul's martyrdom has not faded even up to today. The Basilica of Saint Paul outside the Walls now stands sentinel at this sacred site. Pilgrims and seekers alike traverse the worn stones of this basilica, tracing the footsteps of a man who, even in the face of death, remained resolute in his commitment to Christ.

The legacy of St. Paul's journeys, ministry, and writings lived on though. His letters, now a significant portion of the New Testament, continue to shape Christian theology and ethics. His example of unwavering commitment to the Gospel and willingness to endure suffering for the sake of Christ remains an inspiration to believers worldwide. St. Paul's missionary journeys offer a wealth of lessons and insights for believers today. Here are some key takeaways from his remarkable journeys:

· St. Paul's journeys were fraught with challenges, including opposition, imprisonment, and personal trials. Yet, he persevered, unwavering in his commitment to proclaim the Gospel. His example teaches us the importance of endurance in the face of adversity.

· Throughout his journeys, St. Paul displayed adaptability and flexibility. He adjusted his approach to ministry based on the cultural context and the receptivity of his audience. This flexibility allowed him to effectively communicate the Gospel to diverse groups of people.

· St. Paul's missions extended the reach of the Gospel beyond Jewish communities, emphasizing the inclusivity of Christianity. His willingness to preach to Gentiles and his role in the Council of Jerusalem affirmed that faith in Christ transcends cultural and religious boundaries.

· St. Paul faced numerous dangers during his journeys, from riots to imprisonment. Yet, his faith remained steadfast. His example reminds us that faith can provide courage and resilience even in the most challenging circumstances.

· Throughout his journeys, St. Paul relied on the support and companionship of fellow believers. He established and nurtured Christian communities, emphasizing the importance of fellowship, mutual support, and collective worship.

St. Paul's life was marked by sacrifice and service. He endured personal hardships for the sake of the Gospel and served as an example of selflessness and devotion to others. The journeys and ministry of St. Paul stand as a testament to the enduring power of faith, dedication, and the transformative message of the Gospel. They remind us that the Christian faith is not confined to a specific time or place but is a dynamic force that transcends cultural, geographical, and historical boundaries. As we reflect on the lessons from St. Paul's journeys, we find guidance for our own faith journeys in the modern world. We are called to persevere in the face of adversity, adapt our approach to effectively communicate the Gospel to those who don't know Christ, and embrace the inclusive nature of Christianity. St. Paul's example encourages us to maintain unwavering faith, foster community, and live lives characterized by sacrifice and service. The legacy of St. Paul's journeys lives on, not only in the pages of Scripture but also in the hearts and lives of countless believers who continue to be inspired by his dedication to Christ and his mission to share the Good News with the world. As we navigate our own journeys of faith, may we draw strength from the enduring example of St. Paul, recognizing that the same faith that guided him through challenges and trials can also sustain us in our walk with Christ. St. Paul's journeys may have taken place in the first century, but their impact continues to resonate with Christians today; reminding us of the timeless truth of the Gospel and the transformative power of faith.

St. Paul's legacy extends far beyond his own time, and his impact on the Christian faith is immeasurable. His letters, which were originally written to address specific situations and challenges in early Christian communities, have become timeless sources of spiritual wisdom and guidance for believers throughout the centuries. St. Paul's theological contributions and his letters continue to be a source of guidance, inspiration, and theological reflection for Christians of all denominations. His teachings on justification by faith and acts, the body of Christ, love as the greatest virtue, and the resurrection of the dead have left an indelible mark on Christian theology and ethics.

Questions for you to ask yourself about St. Paul and his ministry

Here are some questions that can help you reflect on the qualities and principles of St. Paul that may inspire you to deeper thinking.

1. What qualities or characteristics of St. Paul do you find admirable and inspiring?

2. How has St. Paul's transformation from a persecutor of Christians to an apostle of Christ influenced your perception of personal growth and change?

3. In what ways did St. Paul's unwavering faith and dedication to spreading Christianity serve as a model for perseverance and resilience?

4. What lessons can you draw from St. Paul's ability to navigate challenges and opposition while maintaining his mission?

5. How did St. Paul's emphasis on love, charity, and service impact your own understanding of compassion and community engagement?

6. What parallels can you identify between St. Paul's commitment to spreading the Christian message and your own dedication to a cause or belief?

7. In what ways does St. Paul's willingness to accept responsibility for his past actions and seek redemption serve as a model for personal accountability and growth?

8. How does St. Paul's life as a missionary and traveler encourage you to explore and embrace diverse cultures and experiences?

9. What can you learn from St. Paul's ability to adapt to various circumstances and contexts while remaining true to his core beliefs?

10. In what ways does St. Paul's emphasis on perseverance and enduring hardships serve as a model for facing challenges in your life?

11. How does St. Paul's commitment to dialogue and open communication with various communities encourage your own efforts at fostering understanding and collaboration?

12. What specific actions or changes in your life can you implement based on the lessons and values you draw from St. Paul as a role model?

Chapter 4: Love and Compassion

In this chapter, we'll dig into one of the most enduring aspects of St. Paul's teachings: his insights on love and compassion. St. Paul's writings, particularly in 1 Corinthians, offer timeless wisdom on the transformative power of love and the essential role it plays in the Christian life. Let's take a look at St. Paul's teachings on love and compassion, dissect the famous "Love Chapter" from 1 Corinthians, and provide practical advice on how to cultivate love and compassion in our everyday lives.

For St. Paul, love and compassion were not merely sentimental; they were central to his understanding of Christian faith and practice. In St. Paul's writings, love emerges as the preeminent virtue. In 1 Corinthians 13:13 (NIV), he famously declares, "And now these three remain: faith, hope, and love. But the greatest of these is love." This declaration underscores the primacy of love in the Christian life. Love is not just one of many virtues but the supreme virtue that informs and empowers all others. St. Paul repeatedly emphasizes that love fulfills the law. In his letter to the Romans, he writes, "Love does no harm to a neighbor; therefore, love is the fulfillment of the law" (Romans 13:10, NIV). He underscores that love seeks the well-being and flourishing of others. When love is at the heart of our actions, we naturally live in harmony with God's moral principles.

In his letters to various Christian communities, St. Paul stresses the importance of love in maintaining unity among believers. For example, in Colossians 3:14 (NIV), he writes, "And over all these virtues, put on love, which binds them all together in perfect unity." Love serves as the adhesive that binds diverse individuals into a cohesive and harmonious community. He urges believers to imitate Christ's love, which was sacrificial and selfless. In Ephesians 5:1-2 (NIV), he writes, "Be imitators of God, therefore, as dearly loved children and live a life of love, just as Christ loved us and gave himself up for us as a fragrant offering and sacrifice to God." One of the most celebrated passages in St. Paul's writings is found in 1 Corinthians 13, often referred to as the "Love Chapter." In this chapter, St. Paul provides a profound and poetic expression of love's nature and significance. St. Paul begins by describing the characteristics of love. He writes that love is patient and kind, not envious or boastful. It is not arrogant or rude, nor does it seek its interests. Love is not easily provoked, does not keep a record of wrongs, and does not delight in evil but rejoices in the truth. He asserts that prophecies, tongues, and knowledge will pass away, but love will remain. Love does not fail or disappoint. St. Paul concludes the chapter by emphasizing the supremacy of love. He states that faith, hope, and love abide, but the greatest of these is love. Love is the enduring quality that continues in eternity, surpassing even faith and hope.

While St. Paul's teachings on love and compassion are abstract, they are also incredibly practical. He provides guidance on how believers can cultivate love and compassion in their everyday lives.

St. Paul emphasizes the role of the Holy Spirit in producing love and compassion in the believer's life. In Galatians 5:22-23 (NIV), he describes the "fruit of the Spirit," which includes love, joy, peace, patience, kindness, goodness, faithfulness, gentleness, and self-control. As believers yield to the Holy Spirit and allow His transformative work, these virtues, including love, become evident in their lives.

St. Paul encourages believers to model their love after the sacrificial love of Christ. As mentioned earlier, he writes in Ephesians 5:1-2 that believers should be imitators of God and live lives of love, just as Christ loved and gave Himself for us. By meditating on the life and teachings of Christ, believers can gain inspiration and motivation to love others sacrificially. Forgiveness is an integral aspect of love and compassion. St. Paul advises believers to bear with one another and forgive one another, just as the Lord forgave them (Colossians 3:13, NIV). Forgiveness is an expression of love and a means of maintaining unity within the Christian community.

St. Paul frequently encourages believers to serve one another in love. In Galatians 5:13 (NIV), he writes, "You, my brothers and sisters, were called to be free. But do not use your freedom to indulge the flesh; rather, serve one another humbly in love." Service is a tangible expression of love and compassion, and it reflects the selflessness of Christ.

St. Paul often includes prayers for believers in his letters, asking God to increase their love and compassion. For example, in Philippians 1:9 (NIV), he prays, "And this is my prayer: that your love may abound more and more in knowledge and depth of insight." Believers can follow this example by praying for a greater capacity to love others. While St. Paul's teachings on love and compassion are aspirational, he acknowledges that cultivating these virtues can be challenging. He himself faced opposition, persecution, and conflicts within the early Christian communities he served. However, his commitment to love remained unwavering, serving as a model for believers facing their own challenges. One of the primary obstacles to love and compassion is human self-centeredness, or ego. St. Paul acknowledges this inherent struggle in Romans 7, where he describes the tension between the desire to do good and the inclination toward sin. Overcoming ego requires surrendering to the work of the Holy Spirit and continuously seeking to align one's will with God's.

As a result of this ego, conflict is an inevitable part of human relationships, and St. Paul's own experiences clearly show this reality. In his letters, he addresses conflicts and divisions within early Christian communities. He encourages believers to approach conflicts with humility, gentleness, and a willingness to reconcile. In Ephesians 4:2-3 (NIV), he writes, "Be completely humble and gentle; be patient, bearing with one another in love. Make every effort to keep the unity of the Spirit through the bond of peace."

St. Paul's teachings challenge believers to extend love and compassion not only to fellow believers but to all people, including those who may be perceived as enemies. In Romans 12:14 (NIV), he instructs, "Bless those who persecute you; bless and do not curse." This radical approach to love exemplifies the all-encompassing nature of Christian love. St. Paul's teachings on love highlight the rich truthfulness and paradoxical element of its strength. Love is often seen as a soft or passive virtue, but in reality, it requires great strength and resilience. Choosing to love, especially in the face of adversity or hostility, is a powerful demonstration of one's commitment to Christ's teachings.

Throughout his ministry, St. Paul demonstrated unwavering love and compassion for the communities he served, even during challenges and hardships. In his letters to the Corinthians, St. Paul exhibits a deep and abiding love for this community, despite the numerous issues and conflicts he addressed. His pastoral care for the Corinthians shines through in his words and actions, as he seeks their spiritual well-being above all else. In his letters to the Thessalonians, St. Paul's affection and concern for this community are evident as well. He describes his ministry among them as being "gentle among you, like a mother caring for her little children" (1 Thessalonians 2:7, NIV). This nurturing love reflects his commitment to their growth and spiritual development.

St. Paul's love and appreciation for his companions are also apparent in his letters. He often expresses gratitude for their partnership in sharing the Gospel and their support during his missionary journeys.

His relationships with individuals like Timothy, Titus, and Phoebe illustrate the importance of love, community and collaboration in the Christian life. St. Paul's writings have influenced Christianity throughout the ages.

- St. Paul's teachings have had an enormous impact on Christian theology. His emphasis on love as the greatest virtue and the fulfillment of the law has shaped theological discussions on ethics, soteriology (the doctrine of salvation), and the nature of God's love.

- Christian ethics has been greatly influenced by St. Paul's teachings on love and compassion. His declarations to love one another, to bear with one another, and to forgive reflect the moral principles that guide Christian conduct in personal relationships and within the broader community.

- St. Paul's emphasis on love as a fruit of the Spirit encourages believers to cultivate love, joy, peace, and other virtues as they grow in their relationship with God. Love, in particular, is seen as a sign of spiritual maturity and transformation.

- The centrality of love in St. Paul's teachings has influenced Christian missions and evangelism. Missionaries and evangelists often emphasize the love of Christ as a compelling reason for others to embrace the Christian faith. Love serves as a bridge between cultures and a testimony to the transformative power of the Gospel.

We have now explored St. Paul's teachings on love and compassion, particularly through the lens of the "Love Chapter" in 1 Corinthians. St. Paul's understanding of love goes beyond sentimentality; it is a transformative force that reflects the very nature of God. As we reflect on St. Paul's teachings, we are reminded that love and compassion are not optional virtues for Christians but are at the heart of the Gospel message. Love fulfills Christ's command for us to care for all people, binds believers in unity, and imitates the sacrificial love of Christ. It is both a fruit of the Spirit and a choice that believers make daily. In our own lives, we are called to embody the love and compassion that St. Paul described. We are challenged to love our neighbors, forgive those who wrong us, and extend compassion to all. Through the power of the Holy Spirit, we can cultivate a love that is patient, kind, and enduring, reflecting the love of Christ to a world in need of hope and transformation.

Questions to ask yourself about love and compassion

These questions can help you explore the profound impact of St. Paul's teachings on love and compassion and consider how they resonate with your own beliefs and actions

1. What examples from St. Paul's life illustrate his commitment to love and compassion?
2. How does St. Paul's emphasis on love and compassion align with the teachings of Jesus and the broader Christian message?
3. How did St. Paul's teachings on love and compassion influence the early Christian communities he interacted with?
4. What impact did St. Paul's emphasis on love and compassion have on the ethical and moral framework of early Christianity?
5. What lessons can be drawn from St. Paul's writing on love in 1 Corinthians 13, often referred to as the "love chapter"?
6. In what ways do St. Paul's teachings on love and compassion inspire you to practice kindness and empathy in your own life?
7. Can you identify instances in St. Paul's life where he demonstrated love and compassion, even in the face of adversity?
8. What role do love and compassion play in St. Paul's vision of building inclusive and diverse Christian communities?
9. Can you provide examples from St. Paul's writings that illustrate the practical applications of love and compassion in daily life?

10. How does St. Paul's emphasis on love and compassion contribute to the broader message of faith and grace in Christianity?

11. What contemporary lessons can be derived from St. Paul's teachings on love and compassion in today's diverse and interconnected world?

12. How can you personally embody and practice the principles of love and compassion that St. Paul advocated for in your own life and relationships?

Chapter 5: Joy in Suffering

In this chapter we'll take a look into St. Paul's ability to find joy in the middle of suffering and adversity. St. Paul's experiences, particularly his time in prison, serve as powerful examples of how genuine joy can be discovered even when circumstances are challenging. We'll explore how he expressed joy in his letters written from prison and we'll provide guidance on how all of us can find joy and purpose in the face of adversity and our struggles.

Let's start with St. Paul's imprisonment as it was a recurring theme in his ministry. He faced various forms of imprisonment at various times throughout his missionary journeys, most often because of his commitment to spreading the Gospel. One of the most well-known imprisonments was in Rome, where he spent a significant amount of time under house arrest. Paul spent a total of about five total years in prison, two and a half years in actual prison and the rest under house arrest. During this time, he wrote several letters, often referred to as the "Prison Epistles," including Ephesians, Philippians and the Colossians. Despite his confinement, St. Paul's letters from prison are marked by a remarkable sense of joy and contentment. This is so hard for us to conceive in today's context, but he repeatedly expresses gratitude, rejoicing, and a sense of purpose even in his restricted circumstances. In your worst of times, have you ever thought about being grateful to God? Probably not. For most of us, when times are hard, we focus on the situation, the world's view of our predicament. In Philippians 4:11-12 (NIV), he writes, "I have learned to be content whatever the circumstances. I know what it is to be in need, and I know what it is to have plenty. I have learned the secret of being content in any and every situation, whether well fed or hungry, whether living in plenty or in want." St. Paul's ability to find contentment and joy is a testament to the resilience of his faith. To see the positive in all situations is a gift and blessing, a gift to St.

Paul and a gift to us if we're willing to take it. To gain a deeper understanding of St. Paul's joy in suffering, let's explore the content of some of his letters written from prison.

The first letter to explore will be the Letter to the Ephesians. St. Paul's letter to the Ephesians provides the understanding how he found happiness and how others can do the same by digging into the theological and ethical teachings contained within its verses. One aspect of St. Paul's pursuit of happiness is his emphasis on the transformative power of faith and identity in Christ. In Ephesians 1:3-14, St. Paul explains the blessings believers receive through Christ, highlighting the notion of being chosen, adopted, and redeemed. This foundational understanding of your identity in Christ forms the basis of happiness, as it implies a divine purpose and connection. St. Paul himself found joy in the assurance that his existence was linked to God's plan, a sentiment that resonates throughout the letter.

Additionally, the concept of unity is a central place in St. Paul's writings. In Ephesians 4:1-6, he asks believers to walk in a manner worthy of their calling, emphasizing the importance of humility, gentleness, patience, and love in maintaining the unity of the Spirit. For St. Paul, happiness is not a solitary endeavor but is intricately tied to community harmony. The shared experience of faith and the mutual support within the community contribute to the sense of joy we can all have. By fostering unity, St. Paul believes individuals can find happiness in the connections formed within the body of believers.

This letter also underscores St. Paul's belief in the role of love in his pursuit of happiness. In Ephesians 5:1-2, he encourages believers to imitate God and walk in love, offering themselves as an offering and sacrifice. By practicing this selfless love, individuals participate in a source of happiness that transcends fleeting pleasures.

The metaphor of spiritual armor in Ephesians 6:10-18 further describes St. Paul's approach to happiness. By explaining to believers to put on the full armor of God, he declares the importance of spiritual resilience in facing life's challenges. The elements of this armor, such as truth, righteousness, and faith, form a defensive and offensive strategy against adversity. St. Paul's acknowledgment of the realities of spiritual warfare implies that true happiness is not a passive state but a product of intentional and resilient living, grounded in the strength derived from God's resources.

The next letter will be the letter to the Philippians, which is perhaps the most notable example of St. Paul's expression of joy amid adversity. In this letter, he talks about his affection for the Philippian believers and shares his own experiences. Philippians 1:12-14 (NIV): "Now I want you to know, brothers and sisters, that what has happened to me has actually served to advance the gospel. As a result, it has become clear throughout the whole palace guard and to everyone else that I am in chains for Christ. And because of my chains, most of the brothers and sisters have become confident in the Lord and dare all the more to proclaim the gospel without fear." Amazing! St. Paul views his imprisonment not as a setback but as an opportunity to advance the Gospel and inspire fellow believers. He rejoices that even his captivity has become a means of spreading the message of Christ. Here he recognizes the circumstance but uses it for Him and with this approach great things happen!

In the Letter to the Colossians, St. Paul emphasizes the supremacy of Christ and the importance of spiritual maturity. Colossians 1:24 (NIV) reflects his willingness to embrace suffering for the sake of others: "Now I rejoice in what I am suffering for you, and I fill up in my flesh what is still lacking in regard to Christ's afflictions, for the sake of his body, which is the church." St. Paul's perspective on suffering is remarkable. He sees his own suffering as a way to participate in Christ's redemptive work and to benefit the church.

Have you ever been in a situation that challenged you to reflect on your sacrifice to others through the hardship? I mean, when times get tough for whatever reason, are you embracing God's blessing and seeing the positive or are you being swept into the worldly view and letting the negatives get into your head? Keep in mind that we each have our journeys to take, but, as we mature within those journeys we must also let go of the old, less mature ways. "When I was a child, I spoke as a child, I understood as a child, I thought as a child; but when I became a man, I put away childish things". 1 Corinthians 13:11-12.

St. Paul's examples here give us insights into how we can find joy and purpose in the face of adversity. While each of our circumstances are unique and our personal tolerance may be at different levels, what we need to understand is that there are universal principles we can draw from his experiences and apply to our own. St. Paul's ability to find joy in suffering was rooted in his heavenly perspective. When we focus on the heavenly world and not the earthly one, we can gain an better understanding and have a clearer picture of the joy He wants us to have. Truly God wants us to be happy and not get distracted by the earthly side of things. We need to focus on the heavenly gifts to come. St. Paul recognized that the trials of his life were temporary in comparison to the glory and joy that awaited believers in eternity. This perspective allowed him to endure his many difficulties with hope and resilience. He believed that God was working in all things together for good (Romans 8:28) and that God's grace was sufficient even in weakness (2 Corinthians 12:9-10). Trusting in God's sovereignty and goodness can bring a sense of peace and joy in all our challenging times. St. Paul's imprisonment did not deter him from his mission, he didn't let his circumstances deter him from his mission. He continued to minister to others, both through his letters and through his interactions with fellow prisoners and guards. Understanding this today in today's context gives encouragement to the idea that engaging in acts of service to others, even in adversity, can provide a sense of purpose and fulfillment. St. Paul's relationships with fellow believers were a source of encouragement and joy to both him and others. He maintained a sense of connectedness with the Philippian and Colossian churches despite his physical separation from them. Building and nurturing a supportive community can help individuals find joy amidst suffering. When this realization is understood, then joy becomes so much more than mere happiness.

Christian joy can be seen as a paradox. It coexists with sorrow, "as believers mourn with those who mourn but also rejoice with those who rejoice" (Romans 12:15). This paradoxical nature of joy allows it to shine brightly even in the darkest of circumstances, offering comfort and hope to everyone who understands. You see, it's written that suffering produces perseverance, perseverance produces character and character produces hope. Hope then can lead to joy. The joy that St. Paul found in suffering is not a fleeting emotion but a profound source of strength. It empowers believers to endure trials with courage and perseverance. In Nehemiah 8:10 (NIV), it is written, "The joy of the Lord is your strength." This inner joy sustains believers through adversity. In 1 Peter 3:15 (NIV), believers are encouraged to "always be prepared to give an answer to everyone who asks you to give the reason for the hope that you have." Jesus himself, in the Sermon on the Mount, pronounced blessings on those who are persecuted for righteousness' sake. In Matthew 5:11-12 (NIV), he said, "Blessed are you when people insult you, persecute you and falsely say all kinds of evil against you because of me. Rejoice and be glad because great is your reward in heaven, for, in the same way, they persecuted the prophets who were before you." This tells us that Christians can find joy in the midst of adversity, not because suffering is enjoyable, but because it is an opportunity to bear witness to their faith and trust in God's ultimate justice.

We have explored the remarkable example of St. Paul, who found joy amid suffering and adversity. His imprisonment and the letters he wrote from prison illustrate the transformative power of faith, trust in God, and a Christ-centered perspective. As we face our own trials and difficulties, we can draw inspiration from St. Paul's example and the principles he lived by. We, too, can cultivate joy in the face of adversity by focusing on eternity, trusting in God, serving others, and nurturing a supportive community. Joy in suffering is not a denial of pain or a suppression of grief; it is a deep-seated conviction that God's love and presence transcend our circumstances. It is an affirmation of hope, a testimony to the power of faith, and a declaration that even in the darkest moments, there is a light that shines.

Questions to ask yourself about St. Paul and the joy in suffering

These questions can help you explore the profound impact of St. Paul's teachings on
finding joy in suffering

1. How did St. Paul introduce the idea of finding joy in suffering in his writings and teachings?

2. What were some of the personal experiences and hardships that St. Paul endured and how did he find joy in them?

3. How did St. Paul's teachings on this topic impact the early Christian communities he was a part of or interacted with?

5. What insights can be gained from St. Paul's letters, such as his Epistle to the Philippians, where he discusses rejoicing in suffering?

6. How does St. Paul's understanding of joy in suffering contribute to his message of perseverance and resilience?

7. In what ways do St. Paul's teachings on finding joy in suffering encourage believers to see challenges as opportunities for growth?

8. Can you identify instances where St. Paul encouraged others to adopt a similar perspective on suffering and joy in their lives?

9. What contemporary lessons can be drawn from St. Paul's teachings on finding joy in suffering in today's world?

10. How can you personally apply the principles of finding joy in suffering in your own life and challenges?

11. In what ways can St. Paul's example of rejoicing in suffering inspire you to maintain a positive outlook in difficult times?

12. What role do community and support systems play in helping individuals find joy in suffering, as St. Paul advocated?

14. How can you use St. Paul's teachings on joy in suffering to offer support and encouragement to others facing difficult circumstances?

15. What steps can you take to cultivate a mindset that enables you to find joy in suffering, as St. Paul did, in your daily life?

Chapter 6: Living a Life of Humility

In this chapter, we'll dive into a virtue that St. Paul both emphasized and embodied throughout his life and teachings: humility. Humility, as a cornerstone of Christian ethics, plays an enormous role in St. Paul's writings. Here we'll find St. Paul's emphasis on humility, share stories of individuals who exemplify this virtue, and offer practical exercises to cultivate humility in our lives.

Humility is an attribute that not only enhances our relationships with others but also paves the way for personal growth and self-improvement. Humility is often emphasized in the teachings of Jesus and is considered essential for the faithful and Christlike life. Humility, from a Christian perspective, encompasses recognition of the dependency on God, submission to God's will, valuing and considering others as more significant than oneself, servanthood and selflessness, admission of imperfection, gratitude and thankfulness and embracing a teachable Spirit. Nurturing humility is a continuous journey. It requires self-awareness, daily practice, and a willingness to learn from both our successes and failures. Humility is not synonymous with weakness or self-deprecation; rather, it's the ability to maintain a modest view of one's abilities and accomplishments. It involves recognizing that we are not infallible, that there is always room for improvement, and that we can learn from others. I once heard someone describe humility as not thinking less of yourself but thinking of yourself less. This is such an accurate description. An actual strength in character! Humility is a quality that fosters healthy relationships and builds bridges between people. Putting their needs before our own is a great way to show others their value. When we approach others with a humble attitude, we create an atmosphere of trust, respect, and cooperation. It allows us to admit our mistakes, listen to differing viewpoints, and be open to growth.

Humility is a recurring theme in St. Paul's writings, reflecting its enormous significance within the Christian framework. To understand St. Paul's stand on humility we'll begin with a recognition of humanity's relationship with God. St. Paul asserts that we all have sinned and have fallen short of the glory of God (Romans 3:23, NIV). This acknowledgment of human dependency on God lays the foundation for humility. In fact, one of the most profound passages on humility in St. Paul's writings is found in Philippians 2:5-8 (NIV): "In your relationships with one another, have the same mindset as Christ Jesus". Jesus, of course being the very nature God, did not consider equality with God something to be used to his own advantage; rather, he made himself nothing by taking the very nature of a servant, being made in human likeness. And being found in appearance as a man, he humbled himself by becoming obedient to death—even death on a cross! St. Paul emphasizes that humility involves imitating the self-emptying humility of Christ. St. Paul consistently portrays humility as a virtue that should characterize the lives of believers. He encourages humility in your personal life, in your relationships within the Christian community, and interactions with the broader world. Essentially St. Paul delivers the message of humility in all you do.

St. Paul's humility is evident in his willingness to acknowledge his past as a persecutor of Christians. He never hid or downplayed his previous actions. In fact, he often referred to his past with brutal honesty. In 1 Timothy 1:13-15, St. Paul wrote, "Even though I was once a blasphemer and a persecutor and a violent man, I was shown mercy because I acted in ignorance and unbelief." St. Paul saw his transformation as a result of God's mercy.

St. Paul's acknowledgment of his past is a powerful demonstration of humility as it shows that he didn't allow his previous actions to define him. Instead, he recognized his need for redemption and relied on the mercy of God. St. Paul didn't shy away from discussing his vulnerabilities and weaknesses. In 2 Corinthians 12:7-10, he shared about his "thorn in the flesh," an affliction or weakness that troubled him. He pleaded with the Lord to remove it but received the response, "My grace is sufficient for you, for my power is made perfect in weakness." St. Paul didn't only demonstrate humility through his life but also exhorted other believers to embrace this virtue. In Philippians 2:3-4, he wrote, "Do nothing out of selfish ambition or vain conceit. Rather, in humility value others above yourselves, not looking to your own interests but each of you to the interests of the others."

To illustrate the transformative power of humility, let's look at some stories of individuals who exemplify this virtue. These stories serve as inspiring examples of humility in action. In the bible there were the following.

- Moses, the great leader of the Israelites, was known for his humility. In Numbers 12:3 (NIV), it is written: "Now Moses was a very humble man, more humble than anyone else on the face of the earth."

- John the Baptist, a forerunner of Jesus, exemplified humility in his ministry. He famously said of Jesus in John 3:30 (NIV), "He must become greater; I must become less."

- Ruth, a Moabite woman, displayed humility in her loyalty to her mother-in-law, Naomi. Her humility is evident in her famous declaration in Ruth 1:16 (NIV): "Where you go, I will go, and where you stay, I will stay."

- David: Despite becoming a king, David, the author of the Psalms, exhibited humility in his relationship with God. He acknowledged his own sinfulness and dependence on God's mercy, as seen in Psalm 51.

- Job, known for his patience and perseverance in the face of immense suffering, displayed humility when he said in Job 42:6 (NIV), "My ears had heard of you, but now my eyes have seen you."

- Mary, the Mother of Jesus, humility is evident in her response to the angel Gabriel's announcement of her role in the birth of Jesus. She said, "I am the Lord's servant. May your word to me be fulfilled" (Luke 1:38, NIV).

- Zacchaeus: Zacchaeus, a tax collector, displayed humility when he repented of his dishonesty and offered to repay those he had wronged. His encounter with Jesus in Luke 19:8 (NIV) highlights his humility.

- The Centurion in the New Testament, approached Jesus with a request for his servant's healing. He demonstrated humility by acknowledging his unworthiness and trusting in the authority of Jesus. Jesus marveled at his faith (Matthew 8:8-10).

In today's world there are more great examples of people who have shown their faith based humility...

- Mother Teresa, also known as Saint Teresa of Calcutta, is renowned for her profound humility and selfless service to the poor and marginalized. Despite her worldwide fame and recognition, she maintained a life of simplicity, serving "the poorest of the poor" with unwavering dedication. Her humility was evident in her willingness to embrace the most challenging and menial tasks, seeing the face of Christ in every person she served.

- Nelson Mandela, the iconic leader who played a pivotal role in ending apartheid in South Africa, demonstrated remarkable humility. After spending 27 years in prison, he emerged not with bitterness but with a commitment to reconciliation and forgiveness. Mandela's humility was instrumental in bridging divides and fostering a spirit of unity in a deeply divided nation.

- St. Francis of Assisi, a revered saint in the Christian tradition, is often associated with a life of radical humility. He famously embraced poverty and lived a life of simplicity, demonstrating a deep reverence for all of God's creation. His humility extended to his interactions with fellow humans, as he sought to serve and love others unconditionally.

- Mahatma Gandhi, the leader of India's nonviolent struggle for independence, embodied humility as a cornerstone of his philosophy. He consistently emphasized the importance of humility in personal and political life. Gandhi's humility was evident in his commitment to peaceful resistance and his willingness to endure hardship for the greater good.

Humility is a virtue that can be nurtured and developed, but it must be through intentional practices. In this way, it is no different than any other characteristic you'd want to incorporate or increase into your life. Here are practical exercises to cultivate humility in your life.

- Regularly engage in self-reflection to identify areas where pride or self-centeredness may be hindering humility. Acknowledge personal limitations and vulnerabilities.

- Engage in acts of service and compassion. Volunteering and helping those in need can foster a humble spirit by shifting the focus from self to others.

- Practice active listening in your interactions with others. Give full attention to their perspectives and experiences, valuing their insights and contributions.

- Cultivate an attitude of gratitude. Recognize and express appreciation for the support, contributions, and kindness of others.

- Seek opportunities to learn from people with diverse backgrounds and experiences. Humility involves recognizing that others have valuable insights to offer.

- Embrace vulnerability as a pathway to humility. Be open about your own struggles, shortcomings, and areas where growth is needed.

Finally, humility is not a sign of weakness but a profound source of strength. It opens the door to empathy, compassion, and reconciliation. Through humility, people can break down barriers, build bridges of understanding, and foster genuine relationships. Humility plays a critical role in the quality of relationships. Friendships are fundamentally based on putting others' needs before your own. Marriages must foster this quality to not just last, but to maintain the covenant that it is. It fosters an environment of trust and mutual respect, making space for genuine connection and collaboration. Humility is also essential in leadership. Humble leaders inspire trust and empower others to flourish. True leaders acknowledge their own limitations and value the contributions of their team members and in fact, put together team members that give strengths to the group that compliments each other. Becoming a humble leader is a skillset that requires much more training in this concept. In the realm of spiritual growth, humility is a cornerstone. It allows individuals to approach God with reverence while recognizing their need for divine guidance and grace. Ultimately, humility is not an occasional act done here and there but a way of life in which daily opportunities arise and are met. It involves a continuous process of self-awareness, growth, and transformation. As St. Paul taught, humility is a virtue that shapes the character and conduct of believers, reflecting the very nature of Christ. Humility is a journey, a path that leads us closer to God and to one another.

Are you one that operates with humanity? Scientists have often studied the trait of humility and have come up with some common benchmarks. Use the check boxes below to help you determine if you are a humble person.

- Self-awareness: Humble people possess a realistic understanding of their strengths and weaknesses, fostering a grounded self-perception.

- Open-mindedness: Humble people are open to diverse perspectives, recognizing that wisdom can be found in various sources and experiences.

- Active listening: Humble people listen attentively, valuing others' opinions and demonstrating a genuine interest in what others have to say.

- Willingness to learn: Humble people approach life with a continuous thirst for knowledge, embracing opportunities for growth and self-improvement.

- Gratitude: Humility is often expressed through gratitude, as humble people acknowledge and appreciate the contributions of others.

- Adaptability: Humble people display flexibility and adaptability, adjusting their views and actions based on new information and changing circumstances.

- Servant leadership: Humble leaders prioritize serving others and seek to empower those around them, rather than seeking personal glory.

- Patience: Humble people demonstrate patience in their interactions, understanding that not everything needs an immediate response.

- Forgiveness: Humble people are quick to forgive and slow to hold grudges, recognizing the imperfections inherent in being human.

- Empathy: Humble people are compassionate and empathetic, understanding and sharing the feelings of others.

- Modesty: Humble people downplay personal achievements and avoid seeking excessive attention or praise.

- Team player mentality: Humble people work collaboratively, recognizing the collective strength of a team and celebrating shared successes.

- Acknowledgment of limitations: Humble people readily admit when they are wrong or when they don't know something, fostering an environment of honesty and authenticity.

- Humor: Humble people often use humor to diffuse tension and demonstrate a lighthearted approach to life.

- Acceptance of criticism: Humble people welcome constructive criticism as an opportunity for growth, without feeling threatened or defensive.

- Commitment to fairness: Humble people strive for fairness and justice, advocating for equitable treatment for all.

- Generosity: Humble people are generous with their time, resources, and support, demonstrating a selfless approach to life.

- Low-key lifestyle: Humble people often lead unassuming lives, not driven by materialism or the need for external validation.

- Consistent humility: Humility is not a temporary state but a consistent trait, displayed in various aspects of their lives.

- Graciousness in success and failure: Whether experiencing success or facing setbacks, humble people maintain a gracious demeanor, recognizing the transient nature of both.

Questions to ask yourself about St. Paul and a life of humility

These questions can help you explore the profound impact of St. Paul's teachings on living a life of humility and consider how they resonate with your own beliefs and actions

1. How did St. Paul exemplify humility in his life and teachings?

2. Can you identify specific passages or letters in which St. Paul discusses the importance of humility?

3. What were some of the personal experiences in St. Paul's life that reflect his commitment to living a humble life?

4. What role did faith and grace play in St. Paul's ability to maintain humility?

5. How did St. Paul's emphasis on humility impact the early Christian communities he was a part of or interacted with?

6. Can you provide examples from St. Paul's life where he demonstrated humility, and how did this impact his mission and relationships?

7. Can you identify instances where St. Paul highlighted the virtues of humility and meekness in his writings?

8. What contemporary lessons can be drawn from St. Paul's teachings on leading a life of humility in today's world?

9. How can you personally apply the principles of humility in your own life and relationships, as St. Paul advocated?

10. In what ways can St. Paul's example of a humble life inspire you to maintain a modest and unassuming outlook?

11. What role does community and service to others play in cultivating a life of humility, as St. Paul exemplified?

12. How can you use St. Paul's teachings on humility to offer support and encouragement to others seeking to lead a humble life?

13. What steps can you take to cultivate and practice humility in your daily life, in alignment with the principles St. Paul emphasized?

Chapter 7: Forgiveness and Reconciliation

Let's take a look into St. Paul's teachings and Christian ethics regarding forgiveness and reconciliation. St. Paul's writings contain incredible insights on the importance of forgiveness, both in our relationship with God and in our interactions with others. Here's the goal, let's take a look at St. Paul's teachings on forgiveness and then move into some practical strategies for reconciling with others while emphasizing the central role of forgiveness in living a Christian life.

Forgiveness, in the Christian context, is deeply rooted in the work of Christ and the narrative of salvation. St. Paul's writings consistently highlight the redemptive work of Christ on the cross. He emphasizes that through Christ's sacrifice, humanity is reconciled to God and offered forgiveness of sins. In Colossians 1:13-14 (NIV), he writes, "For he has rescued us from the dominion of darkness and brought us into the kingdom of the Son he loves, in whom we have redemption, the forgiveness of sins." St. Paul also describes the connection between God's forgiveness and our call to forgive others. In Ephesians 4:32 (NIV), he states, "Be kind and compassionate to one another, forgiving each other, just as in Christ God forgave you." This verse explains the idea that our experience of God's forgiveness should compel us to extend forgiveness to others.

St. Paul's writings contain explicit teachings and practical guidance on forgiveness. Here's some key passages where he addresses forgiveness.

- In Ephesians 4:31-32 (NIV), St. Paul writes, "Get rid of all bitterness, rage, and anger, brawling, and slander, along with every form of malice. Be kind and compassionate to one another, forgiving each other, just as in Christ God forgave you." Here,

St. Paul connects forgiveness with the transformation of character. Forgiving others is linked to letting go of negative emotions and embracing kindness and compassion.

- In Colossians 3:13 (NIV), St. Paul encourages believers to "Bear with each other and forgive one another if any of you has a grievance against someone. Forgive as the Lord forgave you." This verse highlights the idea of bearing with one another's imperfections and offering forgiveness when conflicts or grievances arise.

- St. Paul places a strong emphasis on reconciliation and unity within the Christian community. In 2 Corinthians 5:18 (NIV), he writes, "All this is from God, who reconciled us to himself through Christ and gave us the ministry of reconciliation." St. Paul sees reconciliation as both a divine gift and a calling for believers. He goes on to describe this ministry of reconciliation, urging believers to be ambassadors for Christ, imploring others to be reconciled to God.

Forgiveness and reconciliation often involve intertwined dynamics and emotions. St. Paul's teachings provide practical strategies for pursuing reconciliation with others. Effective reconciliation often begins with open and honest communication. St. Paul encourages believers to speak the truth in love (Ephesians 4:15) and to address grievances with humility and kindness. Understanding the perspectives and feelings of the other party is essential for reconciliation. St. Paul's call to be "kind and compassionate" (Ephesians 4:32) reflects the importance of empathy in the process. Bitterness and resentment can hinder the reconciliation process. St. Paul's admonition to "get rid of all bitterness" (Ephesians 4:31) underscores the need to release negative emotions. In cases where reconciliation proves difficult, seeking the help of a trusted mediator or counselor can be beneficial.

St. Paul's teachings also demonstrate the critical role of forgiveness in living a Christian life. Forgiveness is not just a moral virtue but an essential aspect of our identity as followers of Christ. Forgiveness is an expression of God's love working through believers. In forgiving others, we reproduce the divine forgiveness we have received through Christ. Forgiveness has the power to bring about healing and restoration in relationships. It has the potential to mend broken bonds and foster reconciliation. Unforgiveness can become a spiritual bondage, trapping individuals in resentment and bitterness. Forgiveness liberates both the offender and the offended from this bondage. Forgiveness stands as a powerful witness to the world. It showcases the transformative power of Christ's love and the unique character of the Christian community.

Forgiveness isn't always easy. It can be one of the most challenging aspects of the Christian journey actually. There could even be situations where forgiveness feels impossible or where deep wounds make the process long and painful. However, it is precisely in these moments that the transformative power of forgiveness is most evident. Forgiveness has the potential to heal both relationships and individuals. It releases the hold that bitterness and anger can have on the human heart. When we forgive, we open ourselves to the healing work of God's grace. Forgiveness requires ongoing effort, self-reflection, and reliance on God's strength. St. Paul's teachings remind us that forgiveness is not confined to a single act but is a continuous practice of extending God's mercy to others. In our pursuit of forgiveness, we must not overlook the need to forgive ourselves too. Self-condemnation and guilt can be formidable barriers to living a joyful and purposeful Christian life. St. Paul's teachings on God's grace and the sufficiency of Christ's sacrifice invite us to embrace forgiveness for ourselves. Ultimately, forgiveness is both a divine gift and a calling for believers. In the Lord's Prayer, Jesus teaches us to pray, "Forgive us our traspasses, as we forgive those who trespass against us" (Matthew 6:12, NIV).

This prayer emphasizes the interconnectedness of our forgiveness from God and our forgiveness of others. St. Paul's teachings on forgiveness remind us that we are called to be ambassadors of reconciliation and agents of God's grace in a world marked by brokenness and division. Through forgiveness, we participate in God's redemptive work and bear witness to the transformative power of the Gospel.

So let's take away some practical steps for implementing forgiveness and reconciliation in our lives:

- Take time for self-reflection and examine your heart. Are there unresolved conflicts or unforgiveness that need addressing? Seek to identify areas where forgiveness is needed.

- Prayer is a powerful tool for forgiveness. Seek God's guidance and strength in the process of forgiveness. Pray for the person or people you need to forgive, asking God to help you extend grace.

- Initiate open and honest communication with the person you need to forgive or seek reconciliation with. Express your feelings and concerns while listening to their perspective.

- If necessary, consider involving a trusted mediator or counselor who can facilitate productive dialogue and reconciliation.

- Try to understand the other person's point of view and feelings. Empathy can foster compassion and aid in the process of forgiveness.

- Forgiveness is a choice, and it may need to be made repeatedly as feelings resurface. Choose to release resentment and extend forgiveness, even if it feels challenging.

- Recognize that forgiveness is a step toward healing. It may not erase the past, but it can pave the way for restoration and a brighter future.

We have explored St. Paul's teachings on forgiveness and reconciliation recognizing their deep theological roots and practical applications. Forgiveness, as exemplified and taught by St. Paul, is a central stance of Christian ethics. It reflects the redemptive work of Christ, the transformation of character, and the pursuit of unity within the Christian community. Forgiveness is not a passive act but an intentional choice made everyday. It involves letting go of grievances, seeking reconciliation, and extending grace to others, even when it is undeserved. St. Paul's teachings challenge us to embrace forgiveness as a way of life and a reflection of our faith in Christ.

Questions to ask yourself about forgiveness and reconciliation

These questions can help you explore the profound teachings of St. Paul regarding forgiveness and reconciliation and consider how they relate to your own beliefs and experiences in fostering peace and harmony in your relationships and communities.

1. How did St. Paul address the concepts of forgiveness and reconciliation in his writings and teachings?

2. What role did St. Paul's own experiences, including his conversion on the road to Damascus, play in his understanding of forgiveness and reconciliation?

3. How does St. Paul's perspective on forgiveness align with the broader Christian message?

4. Can you provide examples from St. Paul's life where he exemplified forgiveness and reconciliation in his relationships and interactions?

5. What insights can be gained from St. Paul's letters, such as his Epistle to the Corinthians, where he discusses the importance of reconciliation?

6. In what ways did St. Paul encourage others to embrace forgiveness and reconciliation in their own lives and relationships?

7. How does St. Paul's perspective on forgiveness and reconciliation intersect with his teachings on faith, grace, and salvation?

8. What contemporary lessons can be drawn from St. Paul's teachings on forgiveness and reconciliation in today's world?

9. How can you personally apply the principles of forgiveness and reconciliation in your own life, as St. Paul advocated?

10. In what ways can St. Paul's example of forgiveness and reconciliation inspire you to seek healing and harmony in your relationships?

11. What role does community and the broader Christian family play in fostering forgiveness and reconciliation, as St. Paul envisioned?

12. How can you use St. Paul's teachings on forgiveness and reconciliation to offer support and encouragement to others seeking to mend broken relationships?

13. What steps can you take to actively practice forgiveness and reconciliation in your daily life, in alignment with the principles St. Paul emphasized?

14. How do you envision forgiveness and reconciliation as important aspects of personal and communal healing and growth, drawing from St. Paul's teachings?

Chapter 8: Faith in Action

We journey here by exploring St. Paul's teachings on the heart of Christian faith: faith in action. St. Paul's writings are full of insights on how faith should be expressed and lived out in our daily lives. Living out our faith, showing others who we are, children of God. We are challenged daily to live out our faith by doing the required work…a journey that sounds easy but can be a challenge. Having faith is one thing, but living the faith is a whole other part. Remember, as important as it is to have your faith, it's equally important that you show it as well through your acts. Since anyone can claim to have faith, those who have it willingly show it. Someone much smarter than I reminded me that even the devil has faith, but our works are very different. It is a true demonstration of the faith to show St. Paul's teachings on faith in action and the intricate relationship between faith and good deeds. My goal is to inspire you to apply your faith through acts of service and love.

St. Paul's teachings on faith alone are central to his understanding of salvation. He asserts that righteousness is not achieved through adherence to the law but through faith in Christ. In Romans 3:22-24 (NIV), he writes, "This righteousness is given through faith in Jesus Christ to all who believe. There is no difference between Jew and Gentile, for all have sinned and fall short of the glory of God, and all are justified freely by his grace through the redemption that came by Christ Jesus."

While emphasizing the primacy of faith, St. Paul also acknowledges the role of works as a fruit of genuine faith. In Ephesians 2:8-10 (NIV), he writes, "For it is by grace you have been saved, through faith—and this is not from yourselves, it is the gift of God—not by works, so that no one can boast. For we are God's handiwork, created in Christ Jesus to do good works, which God prepared in advance for us to do." Works, according to St. Paul, flow naturally from a living faith. St. Paul's writings offer deep insights into the relationship between faith and good deeds, emphasizing that faith is not a passive belief but a force that compels believers to act. In Galatians 5:6 (NIV), St. Paul talks about the concept of faith that works through love: "For in Christ Jesus neither circumcision nor uncircumcision has any value. The only thing that counts is faith expressing itself through love." Here, he continues that faith is not an isolated belief but an active expression of love toward God and others. St. Paul often uses the metaphor of the body to describe the interconnectedness of believers within the Christian community. In 1 Corinthians 12:27 (NIV), he writes, "Now you are the body of Christ, and each one of you is a part of it." This imagery highlights that faith in action involves each believer contributing their unique gifts and talents for the benefit of the whole body. St. Paul's teachings on faith in action are combined with the concept of service. He frequently emphasizes the importance of serving one another and caring for those in need. In Galatians 5:13 (NIV), he states, "You, my brothers and sisters, were called to be free. But do not use your freedom to indulge the flesh; rather, serve one another humbly in love."

To illustrate the practicality of faith in action, we turn to the Parable of the Good Samaritan, a story shared by Jesus in the Gospel of Luke (Luke 10:25-37). While not directly in St. Paul's writings, this parable aligns closely with his teachings on faith expressed through compassionate action. In the parable, a lawyer asks Jesus, "Who is my neighbor?" In response, Jesus tells the story of a man who is beaten, robbed, and left for dead on the side of the road. A priest and a Levite, both respected figures in Jewish society, pass by without offering assistance. However, a Samaritan, who was traditionally despised by Jews, goes out of his way to help the wounded man. The Samaritan tends to the man's wounds, takes him to an inn, and pays for his care. This act of mercy exemplifies faith in action. The Good Samaritan, by going beyond societal expectations and demonstrating mercy and compassion, exemplifies the kind of active love that St. Paul promotes. This love is not just a sentiment but is expressed through tangible, powerful actions toward others. Additionally, the Good Samaritan story resonates with St. Paul's teachings on the inclusivity of God's grace. The Samaritan, considered an outsider, challenges societal norms by showing compassion to someone in need. Similarly, St. Paul emphasizes that God's grace is extended to all, regardless of social or religious distinctions.

 There are so many other examples too, probably many in your circle if you look too! Here are some examples to ponder…

- Saint Maximilian Kolbe: A Franciscan friar, he sacrificed his life in Auschwitz by volunteering to take the place of another prisoner who was sentenced to die.

- Saint Damien of Molokai: This Catholic priest ministered to those suffering from leprosy in Hawaii, ultimately contracting the disease himself in his selfless service.

- Saint Francis of Assisi: Known for his deep love of nature and commitment to a life of poverty, simplicity, and helping the less fortunate.

- Venerable Archbishop Fulton Sheen: A prominent Catholic televangelist, he used media to spread Catholic teachings and values, influencing countless individuals through his programs and writings.

- C.S. Lewis: The author of "The Chronicles of Narnia" and numerous theological works, Lewis's Christian faith played a significant role in his writings and apologetics.

- Jackie Robinson: The first African American to play in Major League Baseball, Robinson broke the color barrier and faced adversity with grace and dignity, influenced by his Christian beliefs.

- William Booth: The founder of The Salvation Army, Booth and his wife, Catherine, dedicated their lives to serving the poor and marginalized, driven by their Christian beliefs.

- Eric Liddell: The Olympic gold medalist, portrayed in the film "Chariots of Fire," refused to run on Sunday due to his Christian convictions and later became a missionary in China.

There are even many modern day examples of service…

Jimmy Carter:
- Former President Jimmy Carter, post his political career, has engaged in extensive humanitarian work. Through organizations like Habitat for Humanity, he has demonstrated a commitment to serving others by addressing issues such as housing insecurity and poverty.

Bono (Paul David Hewson):
- The lead singer of the rock band U2, Bono, is known for his humanitarian efforts. He has been involved in various social justice causes, advocating for debt relief, fighting AIDS in Africa, and addressing global poverty, aligning with Christian principles of compassion and activism.

Jonathan Reckford:
- Jonathan Reckford is the CEO of Habitat for Humanity, an organization that builds affordable housing for those in need. His leadership in promoting social justice through practical actions aligns with Christian principles of love and community service.

As we reflect on St. Paul's teachings and the example of the Good Samaritan, we are challenged to move beyond passive belief to active engagement. Can you be better in this arena? Are the opportunities for you to show your faith? Faith in action calls us to embody the love and compassion of Christ in our interactions with others, fostering a sense of community, justice, and purpose. Faith in action is a call to active love and making it a verb and not a noun. If you can't see any opportunities, can you create one? It challenges us to love not only in words but in deeds (1 John 3:18). It invites us to respond to the needs of others with genuine care and compassion. Faith in action is a call to empathy. It encourages us to walk in the shoes of others, to understand their struggles, and to stand in solidarity with those who suffer. Faith in action is a call to justice. It compels us to advocate for fairness, equity, and the rights of the marginalized. The Samaritan's actions in the parable exemplify faith that transcends mere belief. He demonstrates love, compassion, and practical care for a fellow human being in need. His actions reflect the heart of St. Paul's teachings on faith expressing itself through love and service. Here are practical ways to apply faith through acts of service:

- Engage in volunteer work within your community or church. Volunteering provides opportunities to directly serve those in need and express your faith through action.
- Financially support charitable organizations that align with your values and mission. This enables you to contribute to meaningful causes that make a difference in the lives of others.
- Incorporate daily acts of kindness into your life. These small gestures, such as helping a neighbor or offering a listening ear to a friend, reflect the love and compassion that spring from faith.
- Offer mentorship and guidance to those in need, whether it's mentoring a young person, providing career advice, or sharing your skills and expertise.
- Advocate for justice and equity in your community and beyond. Raise your voice against injustice and work toward systemic change that reflects the principles of faith and love.

- Living ethically and making ethical choices in your daily life, including sustainable practices, fair trade, and responsible consumption, aligning personal actions with Christian values.
- Offer forgiveness and embrace the Christian principle of forgiveness by seeking reconciliation in relationships, letting go of grudges, and showing mercy to others.
- Sharing faith with others through conversations, testimonies, and by living a life that reflects the teachings of Jesus Christ.
- Caring for the Sick or provide companionship, or offer assistance to those dealing with illness, embodying Christ's call to care for the sick and comfort the afflicted.
- Practice generosity by sharing resources with those in need, whether through financial contributions, donating goods, or providing support to charitable organizations.

Faith in action has the power to transform so many aspects of the Christian community. First there are the lives of those involved—both the lives of those served and the lives of those who serve. It fills in the gap between belief and practice, embodying the very essence of Christian faith. When faith is expressed through acts of service, it has a real and measurable impact on the lives of individuals and communities. It offers hope, relief, and the assurance to everyone that they are not alone in their struggles. Engaging in acts of service and living out one's faith leads to personal transformation too. It deepens one's connection with God, fosters a compassionate heart, and brings a sense of purpose and fulfillment. Second, faith in action strengthens the bonds of community. It unites believers in a shared commitment to love, compassion, and service. It reflects the essence of the body of Christ, where each member contributes to the well-being of the whole. Faith in action moves beyond boundaries—whether they be cultural, social, or economic. It compels believers to see the inherent worth and dignity of every person and to respond with empathy and care. It creates a wave through communities, creating a culture of kindness, generosity, and solidarity.

Living out one's faith through acts of service is not without its challenges. Think, just a bit, about these challenges, but also look around your world of influence for opportunities and then if nothing shows up, create your own opportunity. Here is a small list of opportunities and challenges to think about and prepare for.

- Personal sacrifice, whether it's giving up time, resources, or comfort you'll need to balance your faith-driven service with other responsibilities. Is there something within your scope of responsibility that can aid others?

- Not everyone may share the same values or beliefs as you and living out your faith through service may face opposition, criticism, or even discrimination. Can you do something that can help bridge that gap? Is there a way that you can help spread your gifts to others understandings?

- Many faith-based service activities require funding, and you may face financial challenges in supporting the causes you are passionate about. How can you identify and connect with suitable service opportunities that align with your faith and passions? Sometimes this can be a hurdle to get over for some. The key here is to find the organization(s) that hit your heart.

- There may be times when you question the impact of your service, leading to doubt and frustration. It can be challenging to maintain motivation during such periods. Perhaps you don't see the fruits of your effort yet.

- Witnessing hardship and struggling to make a difference can be emotionally challenging. How do you re-energize yourself or ground yourself in gratitude each day?

Faith based action may demand sacrifice and it may require stepping out of one's comfort zone and confront the brokenness of the world. Faith in action must be seen as a source of inspiration and not a burden. It inspires others to join in the journey of service and love. It sparks a desire for deeper spiritual connection and a commitment to making the world a better place.

We've taken a look at the teachings of St. Paul on faith in action and the dynamic interplay between faith and good deeds. Faith, when lived out through acts of love and service, becomes a force that not only impacts the world but also shapes the character and purpose of believers.

Questions to ask yourself about St. Paul and faith in action

These questions can help you explore the profound teachings of St. Paul regarding faith in action and consider how they relate to your own beliefs and experiences in expressing your faith through your actions and service to others.

1. How did St. Paul demonstrate the importance of putting faith into action through his life and teachings?

2. What were some of the personal experiences in St. Paul's life that reflect his commitment to living out his faith through action?

3. How does St. Paul's perspective on faith align with the broader Christian message?

4. How did St. Paul's teachings on faith in action impact the early Christian communities he was a part of or interacted with?

5. Can you provide examples from St. Paul's life where he exemplified faith in action through his actions and missionary work?

6. What insights can be gained from St. Paul's letters, such as his Epistle to the Romans, where he discusses the relationship between faith and works?

7. What contemporary lessons can be drawn from St. Paul's teachings on faith in action in today's world?

8. How can you personally apply the principles of faith in action in your own life and relationships, as St. Paul advocated?

9. In what ways can St. Paul's example of living out one's faith through action inspire you to make a positive impact in your community and the world?

10. What role does community and service to others play in the practice of faith in action, as St. Paul envisioned?

11. How can you use St. Paul's teachings on faith in action to offer support and encouragement to others in their journey of faith and service?

12. What steps can you take to actively practice faith in action in your daily life, in alignment with the principles St. Paul emphasized?

13. In what ways does faith in action and service align with St. Paul's vision of a vibrant and active Christian community?

Chapter 9: Building Strong Christian Communities

In this chapter, we'll take a look into St. Paul's teachings on the importance of building and nurturing strong Christian communities. St. Paul's writings are full of guidance on how to create and sustain communities of faith. Let's examine his wisdom, discuss the significance of fellowship and support, and then I'll try to provide some practical tips for strengthening the local church communities.

St. Paul often uses the metaphor of the body to describe the interconnectedness and interdependence of believers within a Christian community. In 1 Corinthians 12:27 (NIV), he writes, "Now you are the body of Christ, and each one of you is a part of it." This imagery declares that every member of the community plays a unique and indispensable role. Just as different parts of the human body work together in unity, a strong Christian community emphasizes the interdependence of its members. Each member has unique gifts and contributions, and when they work together, the community becomes stronger. Just as the hand cannot say to the foot, "I don't need you," Christians within a community should support and care for one another. A strong Christian community provides a support system where individuals can find help, encouragement, and love during their time of need. Just as all parts of the body work together to achieve common goals, a strong Christian community unites around a shared mission and purpose. This common purpose can involve worship, spreading the Gospel, serving the less fortunate, and living out their faith in the world. Finally, in the body, if one part suffers, the whole body suffers. Ever get a migraine? Your head hurts and it can be so bad that it stops you from doing anything else! In a strong Christian community, members are accountable for one another's well-being. They care for one another's physical, emotional, and spiritual needs, recognizing that their collective strength depends on individual health and welfare. St. Paul's analogy reflects the design that God has for the Church as a united and functioning body. A strong Christian community strives to align with God's purpose, allowing each member to fulfill their role and collectively advance the kingdom of God.

Love and unity are central to Christian communities. St. Paul's famous lesson on love in 1 Corinthians 13 emphasizes that without love, all other gifts and actions are meaningless. St. Paul makes it clear that love is the greatest virtue and should be the guiding principle in all actions and decisions. Love unifies people across differences, whether they be racial, cultural, or religious. In a diverse society, the practice of love fosters unity and harmony, helping to bridge divides. Love, as described by St. Paul, is patient and kind, and it rejoices in the truth. These qualities are essential for fostering compassion and empathy in society. When people genuinely care for one another and empathize with each other's struggles, society becomes more compassionate and responsive to the needs of the marginalized and vulnerable. Further, love does not keep a record of wrongs and does not delight in evil but rejoices in the truth. No grudges allowed here.

In our world, conflicts and disputes are inevitable. However, when individuals prioritize love, they are more inclined to seek reconciliation and solutions rather than perpetuating hostility or anger. Love promotes emotional and mental well-being since acts of love, care, and affirmation contribute to reduced stress, increased happiness, and a sense of belonging, which, in turn, strengthens individuals and communities.

To be a strong Christian community, unity is also extremely important. Divisions can weaken the community's witness and mission. We all see, probably all around us, where people are divided on so many issues. These differences are often seen as obstacles instead of possibilities of positives. Christian communities are places of support and encouragement so these differences are celebrated and built upon. St. Paul frequently emphasizes the importance of bearing one another's burdens, comforting the afflicted, and encouraging the weak (Galatians 6:2, 1 Thessalonians 5:11). Let's take a look at a couple of citings…

Acts 2:42-47 (NIV) says "They devoted themselves to the apostles' teaching and to fellowship, to the breaking of bread and to prayer. Everyone was filled with awe at the many wonders and signs performed by the apostles. All the believers were together and had everything in common. They sold property and possessions to give to anyone who had need. Every day they continued to meet together in the temple courts. They broke bread in their homes and ate together with glad and sincere hearts, praising God and enjoying the favor of all the people. And the Lord added to their number daily those who were being saved." This passage from the book of Acts portrays the early Christian community's devotion to the apostles' teaching, fellowship, breaking of bread, and prayer. It highlights their unity, mutual support, and shared purpose, all of which are key aspects of strong Christian communities. Among the various figures who have significantly contributed to the development of Christian communities, St. Paul stands out. His extensive missionary journeys, inspired letters to early Christian communities, and commitment to spreading the Gospel serve as a blueprint for building and nurturing strong Christian communities.

1 Corinthians 3:10 (NIV) says "By the grace God has given me, I laid a foundation as a wise builder, and someone else is building on it. But each one should build with care." In this verse, St. Paul identifies himself as a "wise builder" who laid the foundation for Christian communities. He emphasizes the importance of building with care, which implies the meticulous and thoughtful approach

necessary for community development. St. Paul's message regarding the building and nurturing of strong Christian communities goes deep into specific aspects of community building and all rooted in scriptural wisdom. We must recognize that St. Paul's wisdom is timeless and not constrained by any particular time or cultural context. It remains relevant today, shaping the fabric of Christian communities by providing invaluable guidance and inspiration for communal life and mission.

Strong Christian communities are more than just a gathering of individuals; they are the backbone of Christ's teachings, fostering spiritual growth amongst each other, mutual care for each other, and a powerful witness to the world. The Bible stresses the importance of these communities. St. Paul's role in shaping Christian communities is undeniable as his extensive missionary journeys inspired letters to the early Christian communities and demonstrated his commitment to spreading the Gospel and this has left an everlasting mark on the formation and nurturing of strong Christian communities.

In 1 Corinthians 12, St. Paul discusses the diversity of spiritual gifts within the community and the necessity of each member using their gifts for the common good. He emphasizes that every believer has a role to play in building up the community. In 2 Corinthians 5:18-19, St. Paul discusses the ministry of reconciliation, highlighting the importance of Christians being ambassadors for Christ, reconciling people to God and to one another. Throughout his writings, St. Paul offers practical explanations for Christian living within the context of a community. These include instructions on love, humility, forgiveness, and the pursuit of holiness.

Christian fellowship provides spiritual nourishment and sustenance. It's a place where believers can gather to worship, pray, study the Scriptures, and partake in the sacraments together. Christian communities offer vital support in times of need. Whether it's during personal crises, grief, illness, or other challenges, a strong community stands ready to provide comfort and assistance. Belonging to a Christian community provides accountability and opportunities for spiritual growth. Fellow believers can offer guidance, correction, and encouragement in one's faith journey. Here are practical tips for strengthening local church communities:

- Encourage active participation of all members in the life of the church. Encourage them to discover and use their spiritual gifts for the benefit of the community.

- Strive for inclusivity by welcoming and valuing individuals of diverse backgrounds, ages, and abilities. Ensure that all members feel they belong and are heard.

- Promote the formation of small groups within the church. These groups provide opportunities for deeper fellowship, support, and Bible study.

- Engage in outreach and service activities within the local community. Demonstrating Christ's love through acts of service can attract newcomers and strengthen bonds among existing members.

- Facilitate discipleship and mentoring relationships within the church. Pair experienced believers with those seeking guidance and spiritual growth.

- Prioritize effective communication within the community. Ensure that members are informed about events, needs, and opportunities for involvement.

- Equip leaders and members with conflict resolution skills. Address conflicts promptly and with love, seeking reconciliation and unity.

Strong Christian communities have an enormous impact on individuals and the broader society. Christian communities provide a solid foundation and resources for spiritual growth and maturity for all who are a part. Through fellowship, worship, and the study of Scripture, individuals are nurtured in their faith. Strong communities also offer support and care during life's challenges and trials. They become a source of comfort and encouragement. Christian communities are a powerful witness to the world. Their unity, love, and service can draw others to faith and create a ripple effect of positive change. Christian communities can also have a significant cultural and social impact. Through advocacy, service projects, and partnerships, they can address societal issues and contribute to positive change. These communities are not merely places of worship; they are hubs of love, support, and transformation.

Questions to ask yourself about the need for strong
Christian Communities

These questions are designed to encourage your reflection on the profound impact of St. Paul's teachings and the ongoing need for strong Christian communities in the present day.

1. What are some key teachings of St. Paul that emphasize the importance of Christian community and fellowship?

2. In St. Paul's letters, what instructions and advice did he provide to local Christian communities for maintaining unity and mutual support?

3. How did St. Paul's emphasis on love and compassion shape the Christian communities in his time and today?

4. In what ways did St. Paul encourage the practice of forgiveness and reconciliation within Christian communities?

5. What role did prayer play in the life of St. Paul, and how did he emphasize its importance within Christian communities?

6. How did St. Paul's ability to endure hardships and persevere in his mission inspire Christian communities to do the same?

7. What guidance did St. Paul offer regarding the alignment of one's life purpose with Christian values within the context of a Christian community?

8. What is the contemporary relevance of St. Paul's insights for building and nurturing strong Christian communities?

9. In what ways can the principles and lessons from St. Paul's writings be applied to strengthen Christian communities in our present times?

10. What challenges do modern Christian communities face, and how might St. Paul's wisdom provide solutions or guidance?

11. How can you personally contribute to the building of a strong Christian community, following the example and teachings of St. Paul?

12. Name one solid action step you will commit to accomplishing your stronger Christian community.

Chapter 10: Endurance and Perseverance

St. Paul is known not only for his tremendous missionary work but also for his enduring commitment to spreading the Gospel, despite numerous hardships and challenges. Endurance and perseverance are virtues clearly demonstrated by St. Paul. They are integral to the Christian journey, shaping the character of believers and influencing the growth of the Christian community and the continuation of the faith. St. Paul's commitment to endurance and perseverance is evident if we only examine the timeline of his missionary journeys. From 46 AD to 64 AD St. Paul went on three missions, got arrested, put in jail and then was martyred. The span of his missions, coupled with the challenges he faced, clearly demonstrates his dedication to spreading the Christian message. Here's a summary of the timeframe of St. Paul's commitment to endurance and perseverance.

- First Missionary Journey (46-48 AD): St. Paul's first journey, along with Barnabas, took him to various cities in Asia Minor, today's Turkey. Despite encountering opposition, he persevered in his mission, laying the foundation for future Christian communities.

- Second Missionary Journey (49-52 AD): St. Paul embarked on his second journey, during which he faced challenges and conflicts, yet he continued to spread Christianity and nurture existing communities.

- Third Missionary Journey (53-57 AD): St. Paul's commitment to endurance is evident during his third journey, during which he spent an extended period in Ephesus, today's Greece. He faced opposition from idol makers and challenges, yet he remained steadfast in his mission.

- Journey to Jerusalem (57-58 AD): St. Paul's journey to Jerusalem was marked by adversity and danger, including warnings of impending trials and imprisonment. Nevertheless, he was determined to reach his destination and testify to the Gospel.

- Arrest and Imprisonment (58-62 AD): Even during his time in custody in Caesarea and Rome, St. Paul's commitment to endurance and perseverance remained resolute. He continued to preach and write letters to various Christian communities, providing guidance and encouragement.

- Letters from Prison (Epistles, 58-64 AD): While imprisoned, St. Paul wrote several epistles, including those to the Philippians, Colossians, Ephesians, and Philemon. These letters demonstrate his enduring commitment to the Christian mission, even when confined.

- Martyrdom (c. 64 AD): St. Paul's unwavering commitment to his faith and the spread of the Gospel ultimately led to his martyrdom in Rome. He faced execution, yet his faith remained unshaken.

Here are some strong verses that describe St. Paul's endurance and perseverance to consider.

- Acts 9:3-6 (NIV) "As he neared Damascus on his journey, suddenly a light from heaven flashed around him. He fell to the ground and heard a voice say to him, 'Saul, Saul, why do you persecute me?' 'Who are you, Lord?' Saul asked. 'I am Jesus, whom you are persecuting,' he replied." This encounter set the stage for his life and for him to be the light of unwavering faith and an enduring commitment to Christ's message. St. Paul's missionary journeys took him to various regions, which we have previously covered, where he faced significant opposition from non-believers and encountered challenges within the early Christian communities. His determination to share the Gospel, regardless of adversities, demonstrates the perseverance that fueled his ministry.

- 2 Corinthians 11:24-28 (NIV) "Five times I received from the Jews the forty lashes minus one. Three times I was beaten with rods, once I was pelted with stones, three times I was shipwrecked, I spent a night and a day in the open sea, I have been constantly on the move. I have been in danger from rivers, in danger from bandits, in danger from my fellow Jews, in danger from Gentiles; in danger in the city, in danger in the country, in danger at sea; and in danger from false believers. I have labored and toiled and have often gone without sleep; I have known hunger and thirst and have often gone without food; I have been cold and naked. Besides everything else, I face daily the pressure of my concern for all the churches." St. Paul's list of tribulations is extensive, but it reveals his true spirit and his commitment to the Gospel. The challenges he faced were not obstacles in his eyes, but opportunities for him to exemplify endurance and perseverance. St. Paul's letters are filled with theological insights regarding endurance and perseverance. His understanding of these virtues, in the context of Christ's redemptive work, forms a fundamental aspect of Christian theology.

- Romans 5:3-4 (NIV) "Not only so, but we also glory in our sufferings, because we know that suffering produces perseverance; perseverance, character; and character, hope." St. Paul acknowledges that suffering is an inevitable part of the Christian journey. However, he emphasizes that suffering can produce perseverance, character, and ultimately, hope. Endurance through suffering is a theme that runs throughout his theological writings. St. Paul often uses athletic metaphors to convey the idea of pressing forward and enduring in the Christian journey. His writings state the heavenly prize that awaits those who persevere in faith.

- Philippians 3:13-14 (NIV) "Brothers and sisters, I do not consider myself yet to have taken hold of it. But one thing I do: Forgetting what is behind and straining toward what is ahead, I press on toward the goal to win the prize for which God has called me heavenward in Christ Jesus." This verse from Philippians encapsulates St. Paul's commitment to the Christian race and the pursuit of the heavenly prize. It exemplifies the perseverance that is a hallmark of his theology. While the challenges faced by modern Christians may differ in form from those encountered by St. Paul, the call to endure in the face of trials and adversity remains unchanged. How can contemporary believers draw strength from St. Paul's example in their own struggles?

- In a world often filled with challenges and uncertainties, the power of positivity emerges as the light of hope that guides us through the hard times of life. Positivity is not merely a state of mind though, it's a dynamic force that empowers individuals to persevere in the face of adversity. At the core of perseverance lies the ability to maintain a positive mindset. When faced with difficulties, those who embrace optimism are better equipped to navigate challenges. Positivity serves as a catalyst for resilience, allowing individuals to view setbacks as opportunities for learning and growth. Research consistently shows that individuals with a positive outlook are more likely to develop effective coping mechanisms, fostering the mental fortitude necessary to persevere in the face of adversity. This research solidifies the need for us to maintain the strength to endure and persevere. The mind and body are also connected and the power of positivity extends beyond the realm of mental well-being. Numerous other studies have shown that maintaining a positive outlook can have a real effect on physical health, including strengthened immune systems and reduced stress levels. As the mind and body work in harmony, individuals are better equipped to persevere through life's challenges, armed with both mental and physical resilience.

Let's continue to St. Paul's examples…

- Galatians 6:9 (NIV) "Let us not become weary in doing good, for at the proper time we will reap a harvest if we do not give up." In this passage, St. Paul encourages believers to persist in doing good and not grow weary. He assures them that, in due time, they will reap a harvest if they do not give up. This message resonates with contemporary Christians, motivating us to persevere in our acts of kindness and service.
- St. Paul's letters to various Christian communities are treasures of wisdom on the subjects of endurance and perseverance. Each letter reflects the unique challenges and circumstances of the recipients, providing a unique perspective on these virtues. St. Paul's letter to the Romans contains reflections on endurance through faith. He addresses the challenges faced by believers and emphasizes the role of faith in enduring trials.
- Romans 15:5-6 (NIV) "May the God who gives endurance and encouragement give you the same attitude of mind toward each other that Christ Jesus had, so that with one mind and one voice you may glorify the God and Father of our Lord Jesus Christ." This verse illustrates St. Paul's prayer for the Roman believers. He recognizes that God is the source of endurance and encouragement. Through unity and a shared attitude, Christians can glorify God even in the midst of adversity. St. Paul's letters to the Corinthians reveal the challenges he faced in his ministry and the perseverance required to continue in the face of opposition.

- 2 Corinthians 4:8-9 (NIV) "We are hard pressed on every side, but not crushed; perplexed, but not in despair; persecuted, but not abandoned; struck down, but not destroyed." St. Paul acknowledges the hardships he endured, yet he affirms that he and his fellow workers were not crushed, in despair, abandoned, or destroyed.
- Philippians 3:14 (NIV) "I press on toward the goal to win the prize for which God has called me heavenward in Christ Jesus." This verse encapsulates St. Paul's determination to press on toward the goal, exemplifying the idea of perseverance in the Christian journey. In his letter to the Colossians, St. Paul emphasizes the importance of being rooted and built up in Christ, which requires endurance and perseverance.

While it could be seen as a challenge to provide real-time examples, here are a few examples:

- In contemporary times, the Christian community in China, particularly those facing persecution and operating underground, draws inspiration from St. Paul's teachings on endurance. Facing government restrictions and occasional persecution, these communities persevere through adversity, often meeting in secret to practice their faith and share the message of Christianity.

- Christian communities in regions of the Middle East, where believers face persecution and discrimination, have found solace in St. Paul's teachings. The endurance of these communities, facing challenges ranging from violence to displacement, reflects the perseverance encouraged by St. Paul in his letters to various early Christian communities.

- Individuals and communities engaged in prison ministries, reaching out to those incarcerated with the message of hope and redemption, draw inspiration from St. Paul's own experiences of imprisonment. St. Paul's letters, written from prison, resonate with those involved in such ministries, emphasizing the transformative power of faith and perseverance even in challenging environments.

St. Paul's life is a testament to the enduring power of faith, the call to persevere in the face of hardships, and the transformative impact of the Gospel message. His commitment to Christ and his perseverance in the middle of adversity provides invaluable lessons for contemporary Christians. St. Paul's example challenges believers to press on toward the goal, just as he did, in their pursuit of a deeper relationship with Christ and a stronger Christian community. The virtues of endurance and perseverance continue to be a source of inspiration and guidance for all who seek to walk the Christian path.

Questions for St. Paul and his message of endurance and perseverance

These questions are designed to encourage reflection, discussion, and exploration of the enduring message of endurance and perseverance in St. Paul's life and teachings.

1. In what ways did St. Paul use athletic metaphors, such as the "Christian race," to convey the idea of pressing on and enduring in the faith?

2. How did St. Paul's emphasis on the heavenly prize and the "high calling" motivate Christians to persevere in their faith journey?

3. What are some key teachings from St. Paul's letters that offer practical guidance on enduring in the face of trials and adversity?

4. How did St. Paul's messages about standing firm in the faith and mutual encouragement shape the dynamics of Christian communities during his time?

5. How can contemporary Christians draw strength and inspiration from St. Paul's example of endurance and perseverance in their own faith journeys?

6. In what ways can the endurance and perseverance messages from St. Paul's letters be applied to today's challenges and adversities faced by Christians?

7. What are some contemporary examples of individuals or Christian communities that have drawn inspiration from St. Paul's teachings on endurance and perseverance?

8. What practical steps can believers take to emulate St. Paul's commitment to enduring in their faith and persevering through life's trials?

9. How do St. Paul's teachings on endurance and perseverance offer a unique perspective on the enduring relevance of the Christian faith in a rapidly changing world?

10. What is the role of endurance and perseverance in building and nurturing strong Christian communities, and how can this be implemented today?

11. In a world filled with challenges, how can St. Paul's enduring faith and commitment to the Gospel continue to inspire Christians to persevere and shine as beacons of hope and light?

Chapter 11: Living with Purpose

Living a life with purpose is a universal aspiration for everyone that goes beyond all cultural, religious, and historical boundaries. Having a life purpose is a life target that guides us through our journey that provides direction and meaning to our existence. It serves as the driving force that motivates us to maximize our potential, make a positive impact, and find fulfillment in our day to day. For Christians, purpose takes on a profound dimension as it's intertwined with faith, vocation, and living in accordance with God's will. St. Paul's life and teachings on purpose and its alignment with Christian values are lessons for all to learn. St. Paul, as we have already learned, began his life with a clear sense of purpose, albeit one that was misdirected and not so favorably. As a Pharisee, he was fervently dedicated to persecuting early Christians, viewing them as a threat to his religious beliefs. He believed this was his purpose up until the day he was brought into Christ. Then, once again his commitment and purpose became clear to spread the word. Let's take a look at some scripture now that supports St. Paul's life on purpose.

Romans 15:20-21 (NIV) "It has always been my ambition to preach the gospel where Christ was not known, so that I would not be building on someone else's foundation. Rather, as it is written: 'Those who were not told about him will see, and those who have not heard will understand.'" In his letter to the Romans, St. Paul expresses his ambition to preach the Gospel in places where Christ was not yet known. This ambition reflects his deep sense of purpose and commitment to fulfilling his divine call. St. Paul's teachings demonstrate the concept of a divine call to purpose. He believed that every believer is called to a unique purpose within the body of Christ.

1 Corinthians 7:17 (NIV) "Nevertheless, each person should live as a believer in whatever situation the Lord has assigned to them, just as God has called them." This passage emphasizes that believers should live according to their calling and the situation that the Lord has assigned to them. It reinforces the idea that personal purpose is intrinsically linked to one's divine calling. St. Paul also emphasizes the importance of aligning personal purpose with Christian values and virtues. A purposeful life, according to St. Paul, should reflect the character of Christ.

Philippians 1:27 (NIV) "Whatever happens, conduct yourselves in a manner worthy of the gospel of Christ." In his letter to the Philippians, St. Paul tells believers to conduct themselves in a manner worthy of the gospel of Christ. This alignment of personal purpose with the values and teachings of the Christian faith. Discovering one's life purpose often begins with self-reflection and self-examination. By understanding our strengths, passions, and values, we can gain insights into our unique calling.

1 Corinthians 12:4-6 (NIV) "There are different kinds of gifts, but the same Spirit distributes them. There are different kinds of service, but the same Lord. There are different kinds of working, but in all of them and in everyone it is the same God at work." St. Paul's teachings on spiritual gifts in 1 Corinthians 12 highlight the diversity of gifts within the Christian community. This passage can be applied to understanding personal talents and how they contribute to one's purpose and the contribution to the Christian community. Faith and spirituality play a central role in defining one's life purpose. For Christians, faith serves as a compass that guides them toward God's intended purpose for their lives.

Philippians 2:3-4 (NIV) "Do nothing out of selfish ambition or vain conceit. Rather, in humility value others above yourselves, not looking to your own interests but each of you to the interests of the others." St. Paul says that we must have the same mindset that Christ Jesus emphasizes in terms of humility and the value of prioritizing others' interests. It describes the significance of serving with a humble heart. St. Paul's letter to the Romans offers insights into the process of renewing the mind, a crucial step in aligning one's purpose with God's will.

I am an avid sports fan and am so encouraged by some athletes who are clearly stepping up and have aligned their lives with God's calling. Here are some to acknowledge and appreciate…

- Tim Tebow: Tim Tebow, a former NFL quarterback, is well-known for his outspoken Christian faith. Beyond his athletic career, Tebow engages in philanthropy and ministry work, reflecting his commitment to living with God's purpose in mind.
- Philip Rivers: Chargers quarterback Philip Rivers and wife Tiffany, his junior high school sweetheart, are very active in the Catholic church. Rivers speaks to young people about spirituality and the importance of abstaining from premarital sex.
- Tony Dungy, Retired NFL Coach, is a deeply religious man who was appointed by former President George W. Bush to serve on the President's Faith Council.
- Chad Curtis, Retired MLB. Chad Curtis retired from baseball in 2001, but he was very outspoken about his religious beliefs during his time in MLB. While he was playing for the Yankees, as many as 25 players attended weekly chapel sessions or daily prayer services led by Curtis, the chapel leader.
- Kurt Warner, Retired NFL. Kurt Warner and his wife Brenda are devout evangelical Christians. After winning the Super Bowl with the Rams and being named the game's MVP, Warner famously thanked Jesus, his Lord and Savior, before answering any post game questions.
- Trevor Lawrence. "No matter what happens, I have my foundation," he said on the podcast. "I know who I am. … I don't put everything into how I perform. I'm going to do

everything I can to prepare and play the best I can and be ready every day. But at the end of the day, if I don't have a great day, I've got to know who I am outside of the game."

Are you living for a purpose that is aligned with your purpose? Here's how you can determine that. Use the check box to help determine if you do.

- Prayer and Reflection: Do you often pray and reflect discerning God's guidance? We should be taking the time to communicate with God, seeking clarity and insight about our life's purpose. Listen for His voice through moments of quiet reflection.

- Study of Sacred Texts: Do you frequently, possibly daily, engage in the study of sacred texts, such as the Bible or other religious scriptures. These texts often provide guidance on living a purposeful life in accordance with divine principles.

- Alignment with Core Values: Consider whether your daily actions and choices align with your core values and the teachings of your faith. Living in accordance with God's purpose often involves making decisions that reflect your spiritual principles.

- Service to Others: Do you often look for opportunities to serve others? Living a purposeful life often includes serving others. Acts of kindness, compassion, and generosity reflect the love and service encouraged by many religious teachings.

- Peace and Contentment: Assess your inner sense of peace and contentment. Living in alignment with God's purpose typically brings a deep sense of peace, even amidst life's challenges.

- Seeking and Accepting Guidance: Are you open to seeking guidance from spiritual leaders, mentors, or individuals whose faith you admire. Accepting guidance can provide valuable insights and support on your spiritual journey.

- Fruit of the Spirit: Reflect on whether or not the qualities known as the "Fruit of the Spirit" (love, joy, peace, patience, kindness, goodness, faithfulness, gentleness, and self-control) serves as a guide for evaluating your life and if it's evident in your actions and relationships.

- Integrity in Actions: Are your actions and behaviors in alignment with your beliefs? Living a purposeful life involves maintaining integrity and authenticity in all aspects of your life. Who are you the same person when nobody is watching as you are when people are watching?

- Gratitude: Do you cultivate a spirit of gratitude? Do you acknowledge and appreciate the blessings in your life and recognize them as gifts from God?

- Contributions to the Greater Good: Do you contribute to the greater good? Living with purpose often involves making a positive impact on your community and the world.

The contemporary world presents various challenges to living a purpose-driven life. We've all seen them and are probably already aware of them. Should we look at some of these? Can you relate to any of these? First, there are the constant digital and media distractions that make it so difficult to stay focused on your purpose. Messages from phones, laptops, computers and televisions are often negative in nature and biased in presentation. Next, there is the overwhelming amount of information available on just about any topic that can lead to confusion and decision paralysis. What source are you using to gather your information? While you are looking at your source, I'm sure many others will be present. Can you decipher through all the distractions and mixed media? Materialism and the pursuit of possessions is next and can distract you from a purpose beyond material wealth. Keeping up with the neighbors is a tough battle to fight. Comparisons within social media often promote unhealthy comparisons which in turn affect your self-esteem and purpose. How about the mere demands of work? The work week can limit time and energy for personal passions, add a family to the mix and now your time is even more demanding. Next, there is a sharp increase in mental health issues. Depression, anxiety, and other mental health challenges can hinder purposeful living. All of this could stem from social isolation too. Loneliness and disconnection can deter the fulfillment of social or communal purposes.

Here are some biblical references that show St. Paul's teachings on maintaining your focus through the hard times.

- James 1:12 (NIV) "Blessed is the one who perseveres under trial because, having stood the test, that person will receive the crown of life that the Lord has promised to those who love him." This verse from the Book of James encourages believers to persevere under trial and remain steadfast in their purpose. It offers guidance on overcoming challenges while staying true to one's calling. Nurturing a purpose-driven life involves continuous growth, reflection, and dedication. It's a lifelong journey of aligning one's purpose with Christian values and actively living it out.

- 2 Timothy 1:6 (NIV) "For this reason, I remind you to fan into flame the gift of God, which is in you through the laying on of my hands." In his letter to Timothy, St. Paul encourages believers to fan into flame the gift of God within them. This speaks to the need to continuously nurture and kindle the purpose placed within the believer by God.

St. Paul's life and teachings have obviously left a mark on Christian history. His journey from persecutor to apostle, his relentless missionary efforts, and his letters to early Christian communities all attest to the power of living with purpose. His theological foundations, lessons for contemporary Christians, and guidance in his letters serve as a roadmap to a purpose-driven life. In St. Paul's legacy, we find the message: that purpose is not confined to a select few but is the birthright of every believer. Purpose is the transformative force that can reshape lives, inspire service, and foster unity within Christian communities. It aligns individual aspirations with God's sovereign plan, allowing believers to discover profound meaning and fulfillment in their journey of faith.

Questions to ask yourself about St. Paul and Living with a Purpose

Here are questions to explore St. Paul and the concept of living with purpose. These questions can serve as a starting point for a deeper exploration of St. Paul's teachings and their relevance to living a purpose-driven life.

1. How can one align their personal purpose with Christian values?

2. What role does self-reflection and examination play in discovering your purpose?

3. How can individuals identify their passions and talents in their quest for purpose?

4. How does St. Paul emphasize the importance of walking in good works to fulfill one's purpose?

5. Why is it important to do everything in the name of Christ when living with purpose?

6. In the contemporary world, what are the obstacles and challenges individuals face in living a purpose-driven life inspired by St. Paul's teachings?

7. How does St. Paul's perspective on perseverance under trial offer guidance for individuals seeking to maintain their sense of purpose in challenging times?

8. What is the enduring legacy of purpose that St. Paul left for believers, and how does it continue to impact Christian communities today?

9. How can the principles and lessons from St. Paul's life and teachings be applied to the lives of individuals seeking to live with purpose in the 21st century?

10. Taking all other factors out of your equation, are you living with God's purpose? If not, what is holding you back?

11. Are you willing to commit to taking steps towards living with a purpose that is closer to God?

Chapter 12: Legacy of St. Paul

Let's finish by looking into the theological contributions of St. Paul and the lessons we can gain from his life today. I'm hoping that I conclude this journey by encouraging you to find ways to leave a positive legacy in your life of course, the world around you and giving you the tools you need to live more like St. Paul. Wherever you are on your journey, continue in that growth getting closer to God. At the end of the day your growth will be what's most important. Of course with that growth comes the importance of leaving a legacy. The idea of legacy is, essentially, an acknowledgment of the human desire for permanence. It's a desire to create a meaningful impact that extends beyond our finite existence. It is a testament to the idea that we are not isolated beings, but rather interconnected threads within the relationships of humanity, and our actions can continue through generations, shaping the course of history. On a broader scale, leaving a legacy holds immense societal and global implications. A strong legacy can encompass the intellectual and cultural contributions that enrich our global heritage, from works of art and literature to scientific discoveries and philosophical insights. In this way, a legacy becomes a display of human progress and a reminder of the collective wisdom and aspirations that have paved the way for the advancement of civilization. It serves as a glimmer of hope that guides us toward a more compassionate, equitable, and sustainable future.

We've talked to great lengths about the life of St. Paul and we have clearly shown how he is a testament to the transformative power of faith. His legacy from persecutor to apostle, from a life of opposition to one of unwavering dedication, has left the ultimate mark on the Christian faith. St. Paul's teachings, letters, and missionary efforts have shaped the landscape and continue to influence the lives of believers. In this final chapter, we reflect on the legacy of St. Paul and the impact of his life and teachings.

- Acts 9:15-16 (NIV) "But the Lord said to Ananias, 'Go! This man is my chosen instrument to proclaim my name to the Gentiles and their kings and to the people of Israel. I will show him how much he must suffer for my name.'" This divine calling to be a chosen instrument, despite his past, underscores the power of faith and God's ability to shape one's life in big ways.

- Romans 15:20-21 (NIV) "It has always been my ambition to preach the gospel where Christ was not known, so that I would not be building on someone else's foundation. Rather, as it is written: 'Those who were not told about him will see, and those who have not heard will understand.' St. Paul's ambition to reach those who had not heard of Christ's message showcases his dedication to making the Gospel accessible to all. This ambition is a cornerstone of his legacy.

- Romans 5:15 (NIV) "But the gift is not like the trespass. For if the many died by the trespass of the one man, how much more did God's grace and the gift that came by the grace of the one man, Jesus Christ, overflow to the many!" The theological legacy of grace, as expounded by St. Paul, emphasizes the abundant and undeserved favor of God, demonstrating the central role of grace in the Christian faith.

- 2 Timothy 4:7 (NIV) "I have fought the good fight, I have finished the race, I have kept the faith." St. Paul's declaration in his second letter to Timothy encapsulates the steadfastness of his faith and his legacy of faith in the face of trials and persecution. St. Paul's dedication to his purpose, to spread the Gospel and nurture Christian communities, is an inspiration for all believers. His life exemplifies the impact one can have when driven by a clear sense of purpose.

- 1 Corinthians 15:58 (NIV) "Therefore, my dear brothers and sisters, stand firm. Let nothing move you. Always give yourselves fully to the work of the Lord, because you know that your labor in the Lord is not in vain." St. Paul's legacy here is cemented to each of us as we give fully to the work of the Lord and keep an unwavering dedication to his purpose and serve as a call to action for all believers.

- 1 Thessalonians 2:8 (NIV) "So we cared for you. Because we loved you so much, we were delighted to share with you not only the gospel of God but our lives as well." St. Paul's legacy and willingness to share not only the Gospel but his life with fellow believers demonstrates the significance of building supportive communities and providing mentorship to nurture the faith of others.

At this point, you can clearly see how St. Paul describes his legacy and gives us all clear instructions on how we can build our legacy. With that though, here are some good ideas to consider if you're still in need of some ideas.

1. Clarify your core values, which will guide your actions and decision-making.

2. Establish specific goals that align with your values and vision for your legacy.

3. Consistently act in accordance with your values and principles, in all you do.

4. Share your resources, time, and skills with causes and individuals in need.

5. Pass on your knowledge and experience through mentoring and education.

6. Advocate for causes that are important to you.

7. Dedicate your time to volunteer work with organizations or initiatives that make a positive impact.

8. Contribute financially to charitable organizations that align with your values.

9. Keep records, diaries, or memoirs to share your experiences and wisdom.

10. Contribute to sustainable practices and conservation efforts to protect the environment.

11. Invest in health and wellness initiatives to improve the quality of life for others.

12. Encourage peace and reconciliation by supporting initiatives that resolve conflicts.

13. Speak out against injustice, discrimination, and human rights violations.

14. Lead by example, demonstrating the values and behaviors you want to see in others.

So, there you have it, St. Paul's legacy. We all can certainly think more like him in all we do. Here are some conclusions and key takeaways I hope you got from reading this book.

- Transformation is possible through faith: St. Paul's story demonstrates that no one is beyond redemption, and transformation can be a powerful catalyst for a life of purpose. No matter where you are on your journey, God is there with you.

- Transformation works with action…to have faith is awesome, but having faith means you need to show it in all you do. Everyone can claim to have faith, but those who truly do will want to do more for others.

- St. Paul's commitment to his calling illustrates the impact of dedicating one's life to a clear and noble purpose. Once you find that purpose it'll become your "why" and you'll look for ways to achieve more for it every day.

- Community and mentorship are essential: St. Paul's interactions with Christian communities underscore the importance of supportive networks and mentorship in nurturing faith. Be there for others, in all ways. Iron sharpens iron and it'll be the faithful who sharpen the faithful.

As we reflect on the legacy of St. Paul, we are reminded that each believer has the potential to make a lasting impact, regardless of their past or circumstances. St. Paul's life is a testament to the power of faith, and his teachings offer a roadmap for those who seek to live with unwavering faith and purpose.

Questions to ask yourself about St Paul and his legacy

These questions will help serve as a starting point for exploring the multifaceted legacy of St. Paul and his enduring influence on the Christian faith and the lives of believers.

1. How did St. Paul's transformation from Saul to the apostle Paul shape his legacy?

2. What theological concepts did St. Paul emphasize, and how do they continue to shape Christian beliefs?

3. In what ways has St. Paul's legacy influenced the formation of Christian communities?

4. How does St. Paul's emphasis on unity and love among believers shape today's Christian church?

5. What challenges and hardships did St. Paul endure in his mission, and what lessons can be drawn from his perseverance?

6. What parallels can be drawn between St. Paul's life and the lives of contemporary individuals dedicated to spreading the Gospel?

7. In what ways do St. Paul's letters provide guidance and instruction for believers in their personal faith journeys?

8. How does St. Paul's legacy continue to inspire individuals to seek transformation and purpose in their own lives?

9. What impact has St. Paul's life and teachings had on the global spread of Christianity?

10. What can we learn from St. Paul's legacy about leaving a positive mark in the world and shaping our own legacies?

11. What aspect of your journey can be improved based on what you have learned from St. Paul?

12. What are you willing to commit to in order to be a better student of St. Paul?

13. What obstacles might you come across and how will you plan on getting through them?

Prayer to St. Paul

Dear St. Paul,

You who were once Saul, a persecutor of the early Christians, but were transformed by a divine encounter on the road to Damascus, we turn to you in prayer. Your life stands as a testament to the power of God's grace and the ability for profound change and redemption.

We seek your intercession and guidance in our own lives. Help us to embrace the transformative power of faith, just as you did, and to find our true purpose in serving God. Like you, may we be unwavering in our commitment to spreading the message of Christ and nurturing Christian communities.

St. Paul, you have left a lasting legacy in the Christian faith, and your teachings continue to inspire and guide believers. We ask for your intercession in our own journey of faith, that we may find the strength to persevere through challenges, the wisdom to align our purpose with God's will, and the humility to serve others selflessly.

Pray for us, St. Paul, that we may leave a positive legacy in our own lives and inspire others to seek a deeper relationship with God. May your example of transformation, faith, and purpose serve as a source of inspiration and guidance for all who turn to you in prayer.

Amen.

Made in the USA
Columbia, SC
15 October 2024

44023942R00067